Praise for *Food Theology*

Food Theology calls us to supper, but not before it hands us an apron. With recipes, liturgies, and accessible theological reflection, this book encourages us to imagine how meals can become occasions for satisfying our deep hungers for food, community, and a living faith. Like the meals Lisi and Lohrmann encourage us to prepare, this book is at once invitational, nourishing, adaptable, and best enjoyed together.

—**Mary Emily Briehl Duba**, associate professor of theology, University of Dubuque Theological Seminary

Kellie Lisi and Martin J. Lohrmann offer readers of *Food Theology* a delicious intellectual potluck—historical, theological, practical, political, and culinary (recipes!). The authors urge Christians to "go for it" in congregational food practices: Sunday dinners, community gardens, soup kitchens and much, much more. The helpful "Questions for Discussion" section after each chapter makes this book ideal for congregational study and engagement.

—**Jon Pahl**, Peter Paul and Elizabeth Hagan Professor of the History of Christianity, United Lutheran Seminary

In a world of spiritual and physical hunger, *Food Theology* invites readers to ground their relationships in God's abundance through theology and practices that connect faith and food. Themes include God as a generous host, cooking as a community endeavor, shared meals as a foundation for shared lives, and faith-rooted witness to end hunger. This volume is a guide that will enrich family and congregational gatherings, offering recipes for daily bread to sustain body and spirit.

—**Amy Reumann**, senior director for Witness in Society, ELCA

Food transcends generations and cultures, remains a powerful symbol of hospitality, and brings people together in an increasingly disconnected society. *Food Theology: Nourishing Faith in Local Communities* explores this deep connection between food and faith, offering shared insights on how shared meals can strengthen spiritual life and foster meaningful relationships in today's world. You will read this and find nourishment for your faith.

—**Kevin L. Strickland**, bishop of the Southeastern Synod, ELCA

In a world that feels increasingly volatile and segmented, the centrality of food in life and faith remains constant. Across different generations, diverse cultures, and divided societies, food brings us together. In this context, *Food Theology* is an especially timely, refreshing, and conversational read. It is one part insightful (yet simple) theological reflection and one part ultra-usable how-to guide—lovingly kneaded into a resource for Christian leaders and communities looking to know themselves, one another, God, and their wider contexts more deeply.

—**Savanna Sullivan**, Program Executive for Youth,
Lutheran World Federation

FOOD THEOLOGY

Kellie Lisi
Martin J. Lohrmann

FOOD THEOLOGY

NOURISHING FAITH IN LOCAL COMMUNITIES

FORTRESS PRESS
MINNEAPOLIS

FOOD THEOLOGY
Nourishing Faith in Local Communities

31 30 29 28 27 26 25 1 2 3 4 5 6 7 8 9

Library of Congress Cataloging-in-Publication Data

Names: Lisi, Kellie author | Lohrmann, Martin J. author
Title: Food theology : nourishing faith in local communities / by Kellie Lisi and Martin J. Lohrmann.
Description: Minneapolis : Fortress Press, [2025] | Includes bibliographical references and index.
Identifiers: LCCN 2025007486 (print) | LCCN 2025007487 (ebook) | ISBN 9798889834380 paperback | ISBN 9798889834397 ebook
Subjects: LCSH: Food--Religious aspects--Christianity
Classification: LCC BR115.N87 L57 2025 (print) | LCC BR115.N87 (ebook) | DDC 261.8/32--dc23/eng/20250326
LC record available at https://lccn.loc.gov/2025007486
LC ebook record available at https://lccn.loc.gov/2025007487

Cover design: Brad Norr
Cover images: Wheat stock illustration from AVA Bitter/Shutterstock; apple stock illustration from DiViArt/Shutterstock

Print ISBN: 979-8-8898-3438-0
eBook ISBN: 979-8-8898-3439-7

To Jason, Evie, and Nolan, my very favorite
people with whom to gather around the table.
May you find and create communities
of nourishment wherever you are.
—KL

To Hilde, Jonah, and Theodore,
with whom I have been blessed to share
food, stories, and life together.
—ML

Contents

CHAPTER 1

Invitation to Food Theology

PRAYER

For your abundance, God, we give you thanks
For fellowship, food, kindness, and grace.
Inspire and send us, fed and renewed
By heavenly love and nourishing food.
Amen.

WELCOME TO FOOD THEOLOGY

From biblical times to today, Christ's gospel has gone through real stomachs to nourish people with fullness, fellowship, abundance, and joy.

God's loving care to give people all that we need for daily life appears already in the opening pages of the Bible. Instead of being born into the chaos of a "formless void" to fend for ourselves, Genesis 1 describes God providing for our waking and sleeping, dwelling and exploring, companionship, and even our food and drink.

> Then God said, "Let the earth put forth vegetation: plants yielding seed, and fruit trees of every kind on earth that bear

> fruit with the seed in it." And it was so. The earth brought forth vegetation: plants yielding seed of every kind, and trees of every kind bearing fruit with the seed in it. And God saw that it was good.[1]

From the beginning of time, we know that God loves us, and God loves to feed us with good food.

If Genesis 1 portrays a world created with a loving sense of organization and abundance, then Genesis 2 adds the earthy touch of a creator with hands in the dirt, caring for the earth like a gardener, breathing life and spirit into the new human who will join in the tending and growing of creation. Once again, people and food belong together in beautiful ways: "Out of the ground the LORD God made to grow every tree that is pleasant to the sight and good for food."[2] As these creation accounts tell us, and as Jesus said in his ministry, our loving God truly desires that we "have life, and have it abundantly."[3]

It is possible that these ideas sound obvious, even simplistic or naive, but these are major statements of belief and value that can orient and reorient our entire lives. When we believe that this world was created so that life could thrive with abundance, our focus changes from worry to sharing. Trusting that God provides us with everything we need, we can ask hard questions about what is happening around us that keeps all people from receiving what is needed for daily life. When we see the world as God's garden and ourselves as fellow gardeners, we can consider our everyday actions in light of our call to care for creation and communities. Remembering that Jesus cherished eating meals with his friends, and confident that abundant life is God's intention for this world, we can reflect on these blessings with every bite, give thanks for the

---

1 Gen 1:11–12. Unless otherwise noted, all biblical citations are from the New Revised Standard Version.

2 Gen 2:9.

3 John 10:10.

good food God has given, and pray for ways of living that share this loving abundance with everyone.

Rooted in the conviction that the gospel of Jesus Christ goes through real stomachs, this book invites faith communities to think about how food can and does nourish healthy spiritual lives, focusing on three main points: lifting up and honoring powerful practices that have happened around food in the past, sharing best practices for the present, and building imagination for future possibilities.

This book's title—*Food Theology*—claims the powerful reality that food itself often delivers the good news that the Bible promises: God provided manna in the wilderness, Jesus fed the hungry multitudes, the kingdom of heaven is described as a banquet, and Christ gives himself to all people through a meal.[4] While food is indeed a sign or symbol of divine love and an important physical aspect of God's gracious providing, the phrase "food theology" declares that the food itself is doing the theology.

This is slightly different from the important ways that scholars like Norman Wirzba and Ángel F. Méndez-Montoya have framed "a theology of eating" or a "theology of food."[5] Putting the "food" part first clearly shows that food is an active agent of God's love. Food and food-related activities like cooking, hosting, sharing, gardening, farming, eating, and conversing provide theological content in themselves. The difference between "food theology" and "a theology of food" may seem to be a small distinction, but this book starts with food in order to keep the physicality of eating and sharing meals as central as possible.

In a world of complex longings, needs, and pains, this book also recognizes that experiences of God's abundance are often painfully absent in the lives of many. People hunger for food, safety, health, meaning, and belonging. People come to worship hungry for grace and community. Every day, our stomachs remind us that food is the

---

4 Exod 16:1–36; Matt 14:13–21, 15:32–39, 8:11, 26:26–29; Isa 25:6.

5 Wirzba, *Food and Faith*; Méndez-Montoya, *The Theology of Food.*

fuel that keeps us active, alert, alive, and energized. And, every day, far too many people do not have enough.

While God has created and promised abundance, many things get in the way of receiving these basic necessities. In the face of such deep needs and challenges, it can be tempting to either try to solve all the problems by ourselves or to succumb to the false idea that these problems are so entrenched that they can never be solved.

Between such extremes of saviorism and despair, this book invites readers to consider how one day, one gathering, one worship service, one personal relationship, one meal, one feeding program at a time can be positively shaped by asking what it means that people are fed with God's abundance so that no one leaves hungry. Maybe it means that extra attention is given to sharing words of grace and signs of welcome in worship, that someone meets a new friend over a cup of coffee and fellowship, or that the scary edge of hunger and food insecurity is pushed back for a moment through a community meal. Humble as such things may seem, these daily connections between grace, food, and human longings are at the heart of the Christian gospel. This book aims to address those hungers by encouraging readers to build on existing strengths and feel empowered to live into new possibilities.

HOW TO USE THIS BOOK

Inspiring ways to connect food and faith already shine. Very likely, your faith community has favorite food-related activities that nourish people in body and spirit, ranging from Communion practices to potlucks, community meals, coffee hours, and food pantries. These important ministries and experiences are precisely the kinds of food theology that this book hopes to recognize, encourage, and expand. With a lively survey of food ministries across the country, this book presents a sampling of real-world stories about how church communities have experienced and nurtured holy connections through food. These examples will allow readers to appreciate and deepen the food ministries around them while also inviting imagination for the food ministries that could be.

Each chapter weaves together prayer, biblical stories, theological reflections, faith experiences, best practices, and user-friendly recipes to share a vision of God's desire for community, wholeness, and nourishment for all people. From these theological sources, practical resources, and helpful examples, some readers might be prompted to start a ministry or build up existing ones; other readers might find themselves simply sharing new wonderment about what it means to be fed by God's grace and live into that grace with others. Throughout its pages, this "food theology" book will focus on diverse aspects of God's abundance and ongoing possibilities, even as it directly addresses many challenging realities connected to hunger and care for creation.

This is the kind of book that people can discuss around a table. Everyone has their own experiences with food, memories connected to meals, and favorite things to eat, cook, and share that are worth telling. Each of us is already a food expert simply because of how important food is to our existence. Some readers might have additional insights that come from years spent in kitchens, working in food industries, caring about nutrition, volunteering with pantries or meal ministries, or preparing snacks for community events. Whatever your background, you can bring these experiences to how you read this book, putting yourself in the stories and imagining what could be, or what you might do within your own contexts.

It is also important to recognize that food is both cultural and cross-cultural. Food helps carry the stories, values, accents, and flavors of unique cultures over the generations. The names of the dishes and meals themselves evoke memory, meaning, and love: Christmas tamales, Lenten soup suppers, church potlucks, funeral luncheons, Communion bread . . . the list goes on and on. Foods and meals communicate values, stories, and the spices of life across generations and cultures. One meal at a time, each of us can make the world a kinder and tastier place through generous servings of hospitality, love, and good food.

Meals are often shared in community, and this book has intentionally been cooked up as a collaborative project. While finding a voice for a book written by two people with different styles and experiences presented some early challenges, both authors have come to this project through the vocation of teaching, with many years of experience in a wide range of settings. Teachers often have valuable personal experiences that enhance their lessons without making the class all about them, helping people to learn and take ownership of the material for themselves. In that sense, the authors have found that a gentle, "teacherly" approach allows readers to tie their own aprons, grab their favorite serving spoons, learn a few potentially interesting and inspiring things, and get cooking for themselves.

In that sense, each reader is a collaborator and cocreator with the authors in the exciting field of food theology. You are caring cooks and servers, fellow worshippers hungry to hear a word of grace and inwardly digest it, smiling faces who love to enjoy rich moments with old and new friends. As you engage this material—whether at home, in a classroom, or with a discussion group—it will be helpful to have a Bible nearby to taste God's word and linger in its flavors yourself. Keep a pen handy so that you can engage directly with each chapter, keeping notes, responding to reflection questions, and marking up your favorite recipes and ideas as you go. Like other devotional materials, teaching resources, or recipe books, these pages will benefit from handwritten comments, coffee stains, crumbs, smudgy fingerprints, and tasting notes.

As with this chapter, each chapter that follows begins with a short original prayer, followed by biblical reflections on God's love for this world created for daily nourishment and thriving. These Bible stories can be places for readers to reflect individually or to discuss with friends or peers how food is (or soon might be) a more intentional part of your faith community. Scripture intentionally grounds this book, because God's word is itself nourishing food. As Jesus quoted from Deuteronomy when tempted by the devil after fasting in the wilderness, "It is written, 'One does not live by bread alone, but by every word that comes from the mouth of God.'"[6] The Bible stories in this book are conversation partners in reflecting on and acting upon the daily connections between food and faith.

After some time with Scripture and theological reflection, each chapter examines a different aspect of how food sustains local communities. Chapter 2 sets food theology in the context of the Christian sacrament of Holy Communion, a meal that both tells the story of Christ given for the reconciliation of the world and tangibly delivers that divine promise. Chapter 3 moves from the Communion table to the fellowship hall and outward, celebrating many types of meals eaten in community.

Recognizing the painful reality that hunger rather than abundance fills many lives, chapter 4 first examines historic Christian commitments to addressing hunger locally and socially, then shifts to vital ministries like food pantries, soup kitchens, and other community food programs. Chapter 5 explores the many ways that people participate in God's good creation, whether that be by working in vocations related to food or stewarding the earth through gardening and environmentally friendly practices. Chapter 6 ties all these themes together in a discussion of the contemporary practice called "Dinner Church," which combines Holy Communion, a full community meal, and core values of sustainability and welcome. The book's final chapter, chapter 7, uses words of wisdom from Ecclesiastes to build a vision for all the ways that food both has and will continue to share God's self-giving love with the world: "Cast your bread upon the waters, for after many days you will find it again."[7]

In whatever ways readers might want to try them, each chapter concludes with a narrated recipe or recipe strategy, and suggestions for how to shape a nourishing experience. This opening chapter, for instance, concludes with a recipe for how to make a delicious frittata using leftovers and other on hand ingredients, tastefully

---

6 Matt 4:4, citing Deut 8:3.

7 Eccl 11:1 NIV (1984).

illustrating this book's themes of abundance and creativity.[8] Along with meal ideas, readers will find ingredients and recipes for how to nourish good conversations around food sprinkled throughout the book, including in this chapter. Indeed, while there are many excellent cookbooks, food memoirs, books for group conversation, and theological studies of food and eating, this book humbly attempts to mix these things together in new ways to give practical guidance about how to cook up one or more of these experiences locally. For the sake of easy application in the kitchen, traditional recipes for all the dishes appear at the end of the book in a dedicated recipe section. Knowing that readers will come to this book with a wide range of dietary considerations, some common dietary restrictions are noted in appendix 1, along with simple recipe swaps that can promote safety for people with food allergies. Finally, as ongoing food for thought, each chapter offers questions for personal reflection or group discussion, providing a chance to process the ideas and leave you eager to pass the serving platter as you share your ideas and experiences with others.

Is this a theology book for scholarly study or a practical book for direct congregational usage? It is both, because theology exists for the sake of sharing the gospel in real life, and because living out our faith is rooted in rich appreciation for the word of God that sets us free. As an amazing gift of God, food both describes God's overarching love for us and literally keeps us alive. That combination is what gives value to food theology as a topic to explore and practice. Without presuming to cover everything the Bible says about food, and the many amazing things that congregations are doing with food, or attempting to describe all options that a community might want to try when it comes to food ministries, these pages offer theologically grounded, practical points for readers to experiment with, adapt, and expand. Like a good recipe, ingredients and project times may

---

8 Tamar Adler's *An Everlasting Meal* is a go-to guide for folks who want to keep learning about how to approach food wisely and how to do more with less. Her perspective on food and cooking is instructional, personal, and deeply linked to the ways food nurtures all people.

vary! Readers are highly encouraged to do things in ways that work best for the needs and tastes of their own blessed, God-given settings.

REAL-LIFE RESOURCES: CONVERSATIONS, FRITTATAS, AND OTHER BLESSINGS

Ingredients for a Warm Conversation

Food invites conversation. As an opening appetizer to discussions of food and faith, some simple, open-ended questions can be helpful. For instance, what are your earliest food memories? Are they happy or tinged with sadness? Who are the people in those memories, and are you still able to see them?

Allow yourself to linger in those memories. Perhaps you fondly remember grandparents or neighbors who insisted that you never leave the table hungry. With a zest for serving you, they filled the air with warm choruses of "eat, eat!" Even though you might not have learned their recipes, you probably learned enduring values at those tables: the feeling of being loved and cared for, the challenge of preparing food that is both budget friendly and delicious, the joy of conversation around a table, the delightful smells of a kitchen, and the shared work of clearing plates and cleaning up.

What memories make you smile for joy at the love and nourishment you received with others? These holy memories stay with us. Although we cannot recreate the past, we can honor those good times by considering how to foster rich experiences with the people around us today, revisiting recipes, rituals, and flavors in new settings.

Many of us have also experienced challenging food-related circumstances, including times of hunger, scarcity, hard memories, or tricky relationships with food. These moments stay with us and shape us as well. We can engage these moments in trusted conversation with caring friends, trained counselors, and with ourselves as we consider our own ways of thinking about food and being present at God's abundant table. God is with us in our joyful food memories and experiences, and God is with us in our painful ones, too. While this book cannot erase the challenges that exist around food and eating, the following chapters invite reflection and conversation that may support renewed ways of relating to food. When potentially painful food memories and present experiences with food arise, this book invites you to cultivate trust that God truly desires your well-being and is with you in every moment. As you read and reflect, may you feel warmly invited to bring your full self to God's table. You are welcome here.

Having paused from reading to remember important experiences that happened around food, allow yourself to shift into the theological side of food theology. Take time to recollect your earliest memories about food and faith. If you grew up in a church community, you might recall jostling the other kids to be first in line for the potluck. Maybe some adult watched the struggle to be first and quoted Jesus's words, "Remember, kids: 'the last will be first, and the first will be last,'"[9] which then led to an ironic scramble to be last (and therefore first!). Maybe you remember not wanting to be there, but you were forced to join in anyway. Maybe you remember all things seeming right in your world as adults talked slowly over their bitter coffee and the children left behind sloppy puddles of milk, lemonade, and fruit punch. What were your favorite foods at those gatherings? Maybe it was fried chicken, mashed potatoes, baked beans, or brownies. What about your least favorite foods? Maybe it was vinegary potato salad, Jello molds with chunks of fruit in them, or mushy vegetables. How did you feel when those were put on your plate, and how did you sidestep eating them? How did you join the groups that were eating, or did you feel like there wasn't a place for you at a table?

Maybe you came to know a church community later in life. What was that like? Perhaps something about the tasteful cheese and crackers matched the warm conversation you were having as you suddenly and surprisingly found yourself making a new friend. Some light chitchat over a donut and coffee might have been just enough

9 Matt 20:16.

to make you think it could be worth coming back to worship at this church again. Maybe a meal you shared in a church basement both met a need in your stomach and fed a hunger for having people to eat with.

Through the many memories you have about food, see how you can connect faces, flavors, and feelings: Grandma's meatballs and feeling loved; the kids' table at church and the smell of homemade macaroni and cheese; the warmth of soup and singing a table blessing together. Pay attention to the times you felt struggle and challenge around the table and reflect on what was missing in those moments. These memories are valuable steps in connecting food and faith more intentionally. If you are reading this book on your own, you might make some notes in the margins or back pages for future reference. If you are reading this book in a group, questions like these can lead to rich conversations. Be sure to give everyone who would like to a chance to share their story.

Creating Abundance from Leftovers

Having put our food memories to work, we can give our food imaginations a try. Imagine how the ingredients you currently have around you can be part of your next great food experience. Great meals can come from unexpected combinations of things that were not specifically shopped for and that did not come with an ingredient list or recipe. Indeed, some favorite meals have begun by looking through cabinets and cupboards, examining leftovers of meals past, and creating something new from what remains.

Being creative about leftovers and other unfinished or overlooked items is itself a theological practice. It invites gratitude for what we have and—in the case of leftovers—what God has given us in the recent past. It values the uniqueness of the rich rewards to be had in potentially underappreciated ingredients. It makes something new out of something old. It honors the abundance of God's creation by avoiding waste and cherishing the small things. When we approach our meals with such attitudes, we start to see how the food in our lives is indeed filling us with good theology and blessings from God.

Frittata

Frittata can be one such favorite vehicle for leftover ingredients. With a name rooted in the Italian verb "to fry," frittatas are egg-based dishes that invite imagination and resourcefulness. A frittata always begins in the same way, with the bits and ends: the remainder of bowtie pasta with marinara, some final bites of quinoa that were missed when making Friday's soup, a few leaves of wilted kale or limp broccoli, a lonely sprig of rosemary, a scoop of ricotta from a near-empty tub, half an onion that you sautéed but didn't use, maybe some last crumbs of shredded cheese.

Set aside whatever you have in the fridge and can imagine your taste buds enjoying in combination. If any of the items you pulled from the fridge are raw (such as meat or produce), take the time to cook them in the same skillet you'll use for the frittata. Quickly sautéing any vegetables in a splash of olive oil and a sprinkle of salt will make the final frittata more delicious. Ratios of leftovers to eggs are flexible. To give you an idea of what could be, a recent frittata used half a cup of kale sautéed with olive oil and a bit of onion and garlic, along with three handfuls of leftover pasta, a quarter of a cup shredded mozzarella cheese, and seven beaten eggs. This basic ratio is a good place to begin.

In a medium bowl, combine seven eggs, with half a teaspoon of kosher salt, four grinds (or a pinch) of black pepper, one-fourth of a teaspoon of Dijon mustard, and a hearty splash of milk or heavy cream. Beat this together and set your oven to 350 degrees.[10] Add the leftover ingredients you're using for the frittata to the bowl. Mix the contents well with a rubber spatula, then heat a medium-sized nonstick or cast-iron skillet on the stovetop over medium heat. Once hot, add a pat of butter and allow it to melt and coat the

---

10 All temperatures in this book are given in degrees Fahrenheit.

pan, using your spatula to spread the butter and ensure the pan's bottom and sides are well greased. Pour the contents of the bowl into the skillet, using the spatula to mix, then smooth the mixture out. As the skillet stays over heat, the egg mixture will begin to set along the edges. Use your spatula to gently pull back the sides and tilt the skillet so that runny ingredients come in to fill the spaces along the side. Do not scrape anything off the bottom of the skillet. As the egg mixture takes turns coming into contact with the hot sides of the pan, it will begin to set and become firm. After five or six minutes, the sides should be firm, and the top should still be runny. Transfer the skillet to the oven and allow it to bake for eight to ten minutes. The top should be set with minimal to no browning. Use an oven mitt to safely remove the skillet from the oven. Allow it to cool on the counter for a couple of minutes, then slide the frittata from the skillet to a cutting board and slice into wedges. It can be served hot, cold, or at room temperature. From start to finish, this meal won't take longer than thirty minutes. It should also clear out multiple storage containers and unfinished items in your refrigerator! Frittata is forgiving and, served alongside a green salad or some fruit, quite satisfying for whatever time of day you find yourself hungry.

Creative Nachos and Slider Patties

Another strategy for putting leftovers to good use: should you discover you have a half-full bag of tortilla chips but no eggs, the strategy from above can be applied to make a tasty batch of nachos. The premise is the same: pull out the odds and ends in your refrigerator or pantry and imagine what might taste good together. That wedge of cabbage, chopped and added to already-soft onions and olive oil in the skillet, will sauté beautifully. To this you can add leftover beans, roasted vegetables, or any remaining cooked meat from earlier in the week. Simply chop it all up and throw it into the skillet so the flavors can meld as it all heats together. Taste, and consider what spices it needs. More salt? A splash of vinegar? Perhaps a sprinkle of taco seasoning?

Once this skillet mixture tastes good, prepare a toasty warm base of tortilla chips with melted cheese on top.[11] Pour your mixture over the cheesy chip bed, garnish with whatever hot sauce or toppings you like, and enjoy. The same mixture could also be delicious on toast, over salad greens, or wrapped in a tortilla.

If you *do* have some eggs but aren't in the mood for a frittata, another option is to use the warm mixture to make slider patties. To do this, follow the same steps above. When you remove the mixture from heat, you'll transfer it to a mixing bowl along with a couple of large scoops of cold, leftover rice or quinoa. As a general ratio guideline, three cups of filling can be added to four cups of cooked rice and two handfuls of chopped nuts. A recent batch of these slider patties was made using greens sautéed with onion and garlic, one can of drained great northern beans, two handfuls of chopped walnuts, and a teaspoon of spicy honey mustard.

Whatever you choose to combine, taste the mixture at this point and adjust any seasonings, then add four beaten eggs. Mix together well, then place the bowl in the fridge for thirty minutes or more so the ingredients can chill and meld. Then, warm a quarter-of-an-inch coating of neutral-tasting oil[12] in the same large skillet you cooked the mixture in and shape small handfuls of the mixture into balls. To do this, hold a palmful of the mixture and squeeze tightly. Place in the hot oil. Once the pan is filled (leaving a bit of space between each ball), use a flat spatula to gently flatten the balls and allow them to fully brown on one side for about five minutes. Don't flip them too early, or they'll fall apart. Once fully browned, flip the patties, then do the same on the other side, adding more oil if the pan dries out and scooping out any chunks of mixture that stay behind so that

---

11 A favorite way to make nachos: lay a single layer of tortilla chips on an oven-proof plate or greased baking sheet. Top with freshly grated cheese and place in the middle of an oven heated to 350 degrees. After three to five minutes your cheese will be perfectly melted and chips perfectly warmed.

12 Avocado and grapeseed oil are both widely available neutral oils.

it doesn't burn. Continue until all of the mixture has been fried up into little patties.

Top with whatever you like: buffalo sauce and blue cheese, pickled jalapeños and mayonnaise, red onion and barbecue sauce, avocado and tomato. You can put sliders between any little rolls or leftover buns that might be tucked away in the back of a fridge or freezer, have them with a bed of lettuce, or eat them hot from the skillet.

Whether cooking for one or for a crowd, we often have everything we need to feed and satisfy. We must only arrive in our kitchen hungry and with a mindset of abundance, ready to creatively recast the leftovers that may otherwise be thrown away into meals that will indeed delight and nourish.

CONCLUSION: FOOD THEOLOGY AND GOD'S ABUNDANCE

Food theology begins with the conviction that God created us to enjoy abundant life. This abundance is not the same thing as overconsumption, greed, or consumerism. Instead, trusting in God's abundance means living with gratitude, caring that others experience God's good providing, and finding our place in the world as stewards of these blessings in the communities in which we live.

While theology and religion can often seem full of abstractions, food keeps us centered in the very practical and physical ways that God loves us and that we can care for one another. Leftovers preach the good news of blessings past and present. Memories of past meals connect us with beloved family members and friends who have died or who might now live far away. The rich diversity of food across cultures reminds us that the incarnation of Jesus Christ has sanctified us both in our shared humanity and in the unique flavors that cultures and individuals add to this beloved creation.

The chapters that follow will continue to explore the blessings that come when we receive our food with thanksgiving, savoring what the food is telling us about the gracious abundance of our loving God.

CONVERSATION AROUND THE TABLE

1. What does it mean to you that the Bible describes a God who created people in love and cares about what we eat? How does that belief shape your perspective about food's role in our daily lives?
2. How have you been fed in a community of faith? What is the relationship between being fed in our stomachs and fed in our hearts? What might it feel like to go unfed in worship or in a community? What could it mean for a community to embrace the idea that people "never leave hungry" as a way to describe their Christian faith?
3. What are some ways that food is currently part of your community's faith life? What aspects of food ministry would you like to know more about and try for yourself?
4. Share some of the food memories that you have. Who is in those memories? What is special about them? What do those memories say about God?
5. Like the recipe ideas described in this chapter, what are some of your favorite ways to be creative with the ingredients you might have on hand?

CHAPTER 2

Holy Communion

PRAYER

We give you thanks, O God, for your gift of bread,
Your risen life, in which all are fed.
Turn us in this meal to you,
Hearts, minds, and strength made new
Through the power of your holy word,
The gospel tasted and touched, held and heard.
Amen.

INTRODUCTION: GOD'S LOVE, GIVEN FOR YOU

The New Testament was a meal before it was a book.

While it took early Christians decades to write down the experiences and teachings of Jesus Christ that became the New Testament, the first disciples gathered week after week in those early years of the church to share the meal that Jesus had given them.

According to the gospel writers, Jesus called this meal a "new covenant," which can also be translated as "new testament."[1] However

---

1 Matt 26:28; Mark 14:24; Luke 22:20; 1 Cor 11:25. The Greek word for covenant or testament is *diathēkēs*. Both the 1526 translation of the New Testament

we translate it, Jesus promised that he would be present whenever people share this meal, a gift of life and reconciliation sealed with his own crucified and risen body and blood.

As a promise that is physically received and experienced in the lives of believers, Holy Communion directly delivers the New Testament's gospel message that Christ came to this world to save it; Jesus leads us in the way of God's love by going through sin, betrayal, a cross, death, and hell to give us life with God, now and forever. In a multisensory experience that combines taste, touch, sight, sound, and even the homey smells of bread and the fruit of the vine, Holy Communion delivers that entire story when we gather at Christ's table.[2]

With such deep origins in Christian experience, worship, and fellowship, Holy Communion offers many powerful and profound things all at once. It is the promised presence of Jesus Christ among us today. It remembers Christ's suffering, dying, and rising for us, even as it directly gives the risen life of Christ in the moment. Communion is the grace of God given "for you" in your individual uniqueness and it is given "for you all" as people connected locally and across distances of time and place through the Holy Spirit. It is a deeply mystical and spiritual encounter with God, and it is a profoundly physical encounter with God through the earthy elements of bread and wine. As Orthodox theologian Alexander Schmemann put it, "The Eucharist is the sacrament of cosmic remembrance: it is indeed a restoration of love as the very life of the world."[3] Amid the many things that Holy Communion is and does, it always connects Christ's promises with our real lives.

Describing the transformative power of this meal, Paul wrote to the early Christians living in Corinth, "The cup of blessing that

into English by William Tyndale and the 1611 Authorized Version (also known as the King James Version) use the phrase "new testament" at Matt 26:28.

2 For more on the central role of Holy Communion in the early church, see Gordon W. Lathrop's *Four Gospels on Sunday*, 39–59.

3 Schmemann, *For Life of the World*, 46.

we bless, is it not a sharing in the blood of Christ? The bread that we break, is it not a sharing in the body of Christ? Because there is one bread, we who are many are one body, for we all partake of the one bread."[4] Such words from Paul or a more recent theologian like Schmemann help teach the power and meaning of this central Christian sacrament.

At the same time, asking the young people around us what Communion means can also yield inspiring responses. For instance, a ten-year-old who attended a "Welcome to Communion" class responded to the question of what it means that Jesus is present in the bread and wine by saying, "It means that Jesus serves the world and serves for the people." In a different setting, another perceptive youngster said, "Communion is my favorite part of worship. Because of the food."[5]

The Reformer Martin Luther visually depicted this connection between God's grace and the sacrament of Holy Communion in his 1534 translation of the Bible into German. As historian Gordon Jensen observed in his study of that first Luther Bible, there are four key concepts that Luther expressed in all caps. First, the word *WORT* ("the word") appears in capital letters in Wisdom of Solomon 16:12 and 18:22, to emphasize the power of God's word to heal and liberate all people.[6] Next, Luther capitalized "LISTEN TO HIM" in the transfiguration accounts of Matthew, Mark, and Luke[7] to connect this healing word with Jesus Christ. The third capitalization appears at Romans 3:25 with the words "FORGIVES SIN," as Luther believed that the forgiveness of sins summarized

4 1 Cor 10:16–17.

5 Both quotations from young people have been shared with permission.

6 Jensen, *Experiencing Gospel*, 83; Wis 16:12: "For neither herb nor poultice cured them, but it was your word, O Lord, that heals all people," 18:22: "He conquered the wrath not by strength of body, not by force of arms, but by his word he subdued the avenger, appealing to the oaths and covenants given to our ancestors."

7 Jensen, 98, referring to Matt 17:5; Mark 9:7; Luke 9:35.

the gospel's holistic work to save, free, reconcile, and restore this broken world.[8]

Finally, the fourth instance of capitalization is the word "TAKE" in Paul's account of the institution of the Lord's Supper in 1 Corinthians 11. Jensen wrote, "Luther wanted to emphasize that the 'sacrament is a visible Word' and that in the Lord's Supper, nothing but gospel is heard and seen."[9] Indeed, the entire gospel of Christ's saving action to be born, live among us, die, and rise for us, is seen, heard, and tasted in this sacrament. Jensen's study has shown how the text of the first Luther Bible vividly illustrates the power of food to bear and share the Christian message. For Luther, taking hold of the sacrament in both body and faith meant receiving the promises of God into one's very self. Through the word "TAKE," Luther showed that the food itself delivers, bears, and is itself nourishment from God.

HOLY COMMUNION AND FOOD THEOLOGY

At Rainbow Trail, an outdoor camp ministry in Colorado, Saturday Communion marks the culmination of a week full of literal and figurative mountaintop experiences. Once cabins are cleaned, the final meal eaten, the closing worship shared, the last tearful goodbye said, and once every camper has been picked up by their adults, the staff gathers to return to their own collective community. Weary, relieved, a little bit heartbroken from the goodbyes, and ready for their time off, the staff circles on the grass to share their joys and challenges from the week. In this weekly ritual, the entire staff is physically and emotionally drawn together as an embodied community, which includes the practice of Holy Communion. Still in a circle, the staff community participates in a eucharistic liturgy, giving thanks and hearing the familiar story of Jesus breaking the bread, giving himself to his friends, and promising his very body and lifeblood

8 Jensen, 116.

9 Jensen, 137.

to them. Led by an ordained presider, the group prays the familiar words of the Lord's Prayer knowing that, just like them, Jesus walked earth's hills and valleys, spent time with his friends, cried tears of loss and grief, prayed in both good and troubled moments, slept on the ground, and experienced the amazing gifts and enduring challenges of life in community. The bread and wine are given for each of them, and in that meal the staff experiences the tangible promise of Jesus and an entrance into the story of God's own self, poured out in service and care for the well-being of all creation. It is a beautiful and nourishing experience.

In a different context, author and minister Sara Miles reflected on the holy transformation that happens through Holy Communion in her book *Take This Bread*. Not raised in a church, Miles found herself surprisingly drawn to the Eucharist as an adult, recalling how "someone was putting a piece of fresh, crumbly bread in my hands, saying 'the body of Christ,' and handing me the goblet of sweet wine, saying 'the blood of Christ,' and then something outrageous and terrifying happened. Jesus happened to me."[10] The self-giving Lord of life personally appeared through the bread and wine, inspiring Miles to build new connections through food and faith in her community.

Whether in the remote environs of a camp or the hustle and bustle of Sara Miles's city contexts, Jesus happens to us every time we partake in his meal. Whether celebrated around a Communion rail, at a work site, in the mountains, in a hospital room, or on the side of the road, the experience and practice of Holy Communion connects us with the triune God and with each other. The eucharistic meal does not take us out of the world but rather joins us to it with the incarnational love of Christ.

Food theology, then, begins with God's care for us as the beloved, embodied creatures that we are as members of this good creation. In Holy Communion, physical realities like bread and wine offer a tangible, tastable encounter with our loving Lord. In this central moment of Christ's promise and presence, we find ourselves

---

10 Miles, *Take This Bread*, 58.

connected and reconnected to God and each other in all kinds of ways. The hands that grew the grain, tended the grapes, baked the bread, set the table, and served the elements are part of this promise. The land that provides such essential nourishment is holy and blessed. The workers who have brought us such blessed food and drink are part of this story. The people around us are not strangers but fellow travelers on the journey of faith. Hearts nourished by this meal go out strengthened to serve everyone they meet. After Communion, we carry this experience of unity, grace, and reconciliation with us wherever we go, enriched by the abundant life of God that we receive in the Lord's Supper.

At the same time, the deep spiritual experience and meaning of Holy Communion can sometimes make it feel far away from the rest of our lives. For instance, this meal happens at an unusual piece of furniture called an altar. A religious professional like a priest or pastor leads the congregation through words and prayers that are almost two thousand years old. Some people might kneel to receive the bread and the cup. Other people might make the sign of the cross or quietly pray. Tears may be shed. Songs might be sung in spirits of joy, or contemplation, or both, or not at all. So many religiously significant things are happening during Communion that it might feel like the sacrament—itself a word that means "mystery"—is shrouded in a far-off holiness that we really should not investigate, explore, or talk about outside of church.

It can be helpful, therefore, to keep things simple when we think about how to celebrate the Lord's Supper, with basic issues of hospitality providing good starting points for sharing Communion with fullness and joy. For instance, will guests be able to participate in Communion with relative ease, knowing when, how, or where to receive the elements? Will children be invited to commune or be encouraged to take part in other ways? Are options provided for people who have wheat allergies or who do not drink alcohol?

As Sara Miles's reflection shows, imagining what this experience might be like from the perspective of a newcomer can benefit everyone who participates. Thinking in advance about how to be clear, welcoming, and hospitable when it comes to sharing this sacrament is an act of food theology. Newcomers, guests, and visitors will all feel valued by knowing that their experience has been considered by those planning worship. Longtime members will be encouraged to remember for themselves the ongoing blessing of the body of Christ when they think about it from the perspective of those who might be communing for the first time in a new place. Indeed, the power of words and experiences like commune, unity, community, and communion all take on renewed vitality and significance when we recall that every gathering around the Lord's table is a fresh moment of belonging to the "communion of saints."

ELEMENTS OF THE EUCHARIST

Because the physical elements of the bread and the cup are themselves bearing the grace of God, they provide a wonderful starting point for considering how to share the holy simplicity of Communion. While there are many worthy options when it comes to deciding what bread and wine to serve—wafers or loaves, wine or nonalcoholic grape juice, elements made locally or shipped from elsewhere, and so on—it can be enjoyable and helpful for a congregation to think about what it serves and why. Does a single loaf of bread communicate Christian unity better than wafers, or do wafers provide advantages to those who prepare, serve, and receive Communion? Are there manageable ways for bread to be baked by the community or purchased locally? How are people with dietary restrictions such as gluten intolerance or other food allergies welcomed to the table, and what bread is available for them to safely consume? These are important conversations that can be both enjoyable to engage in as a community and important to consider with intentionality.

When it comes to thinking about what is served at Communion, some churches have discovered that serving grape juice or nonalcoholic wine helped support their ministries with people in recovery from substance abuse addictions. Pastor Joe Ellwanger, for instance, found that "The very fact that we offered grape juice was a signal to everyone in the recovery community that we really cared about them and about their tough day-to-day battle with substance abuse addiction. It also signaled to people who did not have that struggle that they should be concerned about those who do have that struggle to deal with."[11] Although wine rather than grape juice has been the traditional element used in Holy Communion, the promises of the sacrament do not depend on that choice. Instead, Communion elements that communicate grace to the gathered community are what matter most. As Lorraine Brugh and Gordon Lathrop have written, "The bread and wine should be straightforward, simply beautiful and tasty, basic, recognizable human food, but not things that call attention to themselves."[12]

At the end of this chapter, you will find two bread recipes which fulfill the characteristics named by Brugh and Lathrop: one is a gluten-free, soy-free, nut-free, vegan bread that can work well for congregations that desire to be as dietarily inclusive as possible. The other is a bread made with all-purpose flour and molasses, which is invitational in its simplicity and heartiness. As with wafers or store-bought bread, both can fully communicate the nourishing love and reconciling grace of the triune God in your community.

EXPERIENCING EUCHARIST

While the elements of Holy Communion do much to enrich the theology of the sacrament, so too does the experience of receiving Holy Communion express the theology; the experience of Holy Communion does much to shape our beliefs and understanding of who God is and how God shows up with us. Throughout this book we will explore new ways of living and eating together as we consider the

11 Ellwanger, *Strength for the Struggle*, 179.

12 Brugh and Lathrop, *The Sunday Assembly*, 190. For more on this discussion, see Brugh and Lathrop, 187–194.

transformative act of gathering people around food. This exploration begins with an attunement to how we celebrate and participate in the Eucharist, considering the very experience of Holy Communion as a conveyance of our theology just as much as the words that are spoken and the elements that are blessed.

Because Communion is about our relationship with God, it is important to think about how to let people know that they matter to God and that they belong. You are invited to reflect on this point and start imagining or remembering different ways that you have felt both invited into a community and excluded from one. What practices and attitudes let you know that you were welcome? What things made you feel like an outsider at church or the Communion table? How might you build on these insights in a way that could help a visitor feel more welcome?

The question of who is invited to the table is another important theological tenet to consider in prayerful conversation and reflection. Some faith communities have clear expectations that define who can receive Communion and who should not or cannot. Many of these expectations exist because Communion is so important that the congregation wants people to know what is happening and why it matters so much. In those communities, expectations can be experienced graciously when church members share their values and invite newcomers to get to know this central part of their life together. In other situations, though, limits on who can receive Communion can be experienced as exclusionary, even painfully so.

In many cases, historical divisions are responsible for different faith traditions having literally "fallen out of communion" with each other, as in the lack of communion fellowship between ancient branches of the church like Roman Catholicism and Eastern Orthodoxy that has existed since the "Great Schism" of 1054. Many communities rooted in the Protestant Reformation of the 1500s have also been out of communion with each other over the centuries because of differing views of what the sacrament means and the role it plays in Christian life.

These divisions reflect the reality of brokenness within Christ's one church. And yet, just as Jesus shared his Last Supper with friends who would soon fail their time of trial, there is a way in which these human shortcomings nevertheless testify to the all-embracing love of God. Even as human boundaries continue to divide, the Holy Spirit is at work through and beyond our limitations, guiding and enriching our understanding of the triune God through the differing, unique values about Holy Communion that are held by various faith traditions.

In Eastern Orthodoxy, for example, the Eucharist is the beginning and the goal of all life; it is God's love for creation, shared freely, for the transformation of the world. To participate in the Eucharist in the Orthodox tradition is to be part of God's joyous gift of creation, redemption, and sanctification given through Jesus Christ. Roman Catholicism similarly values the Eucharist for the unity in faith it affirms and for the way that it physically brings the grace of God to a world that desperately needs it.

Among Protestants, Lutherans share the Catholic belief that Christ is truly present in the Communion elements, emphasizing the "for you" aspect of what God is giving in Communion, received in body and in faith. Reformed Protestants value Holy Communion as a sign of Christian unity, as a remembrance of Christ's saving work, and as spiritual communion with God and each other. Churches of the Anglican Communion made space for both the Catholic and Reformed perspectives by focusing on the unity that comes from sharing the words and actions of the Eucharist. Other branches of the Reformation like Moravians, Mennonites, and Methodists celebrate a love feast as a way to live into the harmony promised by Jesus through this meal. The Christian Church (Disciples of Christ) sees the act of sharing Communion as itself being the amazing gift of God that overcomes all that would keep us from the unity we share in Christ.

Throughout Christ's church (and churches), the importance of the experience of Holy Communion is affirmed, even as it is celebrated with different elements, practices, and considerations. One consideration that many faith communities wrestle with is the question of what age children might start receiving Communion. Some church bodies commune children as soon as they can reach out and taste the elements. This practice lets everyone know that children are valued and included in a fundamental way in the congregation. It can also foster a healthy sense of belonging and a hunger to receive Communion at a young age. A community can then build on this experience with intentional teaching about Holy Communion in lifelong Christian education.

Communities that wait until young people have been instructed about the meaning and significance of Eucharist are also valuing their youth by letting them know the importance of this central Christian meal. Children can be included in the Eucharist in other ways, for instance, by coming forward for a blessing at the table. Just as with all decisions being made around the sacrament of Holy Communion, the most important point is to consider how the local practices are communicating the love of God as proclaimed through Christ who gave his own body and blood so that all people might have life in him.

In the words of the late South African theologian David Bosch, the church exists to share "God's self-revelation as the One who loves the world."[13] Holy Communion is not only a symbol of that love but an experience of and participation in it. It is the New Testament we can touch, taste, and eat. Like the disciples who denied and abandoned Jesus "on the night he was betrayed," we come to the Lord's table with shortcomings, sins, fears, and failures. Knowing this about us, Jesus continues to set a table and feed us with this meal of grace, forgiveness, reconciliation, strength, and courage. In Communion we are united with God in Christ Jesus who, by the power of the Holy Spirit, knits us together into one body, one loaf, so that all may be fed and nourished. No matter how or where or when we eat, this Holy Communion is at the heart of our experience with both food and theology.

---

13 Bosch, *Transforming Mission*, 10.

The goal of sharing Jesus's grace with others as clearly as possible—in word, deed, and meal—is worth our time and effort. At the same time, the Lord's Supper doesn't depend on us getting everything "just right." We are free to let the Holy Spirit bring grace to us, truly receiving it from God as a gift. As Martin Luther wrote in his *Large Catechism* about feeling unworthy or not good enough to receive Communion, "People with such misgivings must learn that it is the highest art to realize that this sacrament does not depend on our worthiness. For we are not baptized because we are holy or worthy, nor do we come to confession as if we were pure and without sin; on the contrary, we come as poor, miserable people, precisely because we are unworthy."[14] In this light, the best way to receive and share Communion is with honesty about our broken lives and to trust even more in God's good care for us and among us, including in our time together at Christ's table.

In Holy Communion, Jesus gave us a meal that forgives and unites, connecting the promises of God with our physical bodies as we are handed the bread and cup and told: "The body of Christ given for you. The blood of Christ shed for you." Beyond the presider, the liturgy, the people, the elements, in Holy Communion we understand that the food itself communicates all that this simultaneously heavenly and earthly meal wants to give us. Made powerful through the promises of God, the food itself is doing the theology. The New Testament is a meal.

REAL-LIFE RESOURCES: BAKING COMMUNION BREAD TOGETHER

Baking Communion bread together can provide a wonderful way to engage the sacrament as a community of faith. In this practice—which will be the focus of the rest of this chapter—hands go to work, conversations grow while stirring ingredients, and new relationships

14 Kolb and Wengert, *The Book of Concord* [hereafter abbreviated *BC*], 473.

rise like fresh bread. Readers are welcome to follow or adapt the outline below as they see fit, as each section presents opportunities for learning, service, and fellowship.

Baking Communion bread together includes the following steps:

- Shopping and preparing to cook
- Gathering, with introductions and conversation starters
- Mixing, baking, and talking
- Making the sign of the cross, and discussing its meaning
- Preparing for worship, cleaning, and sending

This outline can provide a good basis for small group gatherings, confirmation class, intergenerational experiences, or personal devotion.

Shopping and Preparing

Baking begins with gathering the ingredients and utensils together. While that might sound less than thrilling, shopping for ingredients can be a great activity for members of a youth group to learn some new practical skills and have fun together. It can also be a devotional act for church members who serve their congregations in this way. When shopping, it is helpful to know in advance who is paying. Because Communion bread is a part of worship, it is reasonable for the church to cover or reimburse the costs fully. Alternatively, someone in the congregation might want to make paying for the ingredients part of their donation to the church for a time. Keeping receipts can be helpful for recording expenses and donations.

Two recipes with lists of ingredients are provided in the recipe section of this book. They can be adapted or shared with attribution. The first recipe is slightly simpler and contains gluten. It is user friendly and comes out well for people with all ranges of cooking experience. The second recipe is free of allergens including wheat, dairy, nuts, eggs, soy, and xanthan gum. Like the first recipe, it is delicious and breaks apart easily for Communion distribution during worship. Planners of the bread-baking event are welcome to choose the recipe that works best for their community, and maybe even try both, taking care to avoid cross contamination for the sake of those with allergies.

The recipes offered also include lists of utensils: mixing bowls, whisks, spatulas, baking pans, and the like. Again, the congregation should take the lead responsibility for providing these items, either by sharing kitchen equipment or buying needed supplies. If some people—for instance, the organizers of the bread-baking event—need to bring their own equipment, then these items should be labeled so that nothing gets lost, because caring for people's possessions is a way to show respect for each other and nurture an environment of joyful giving and receiving. Also, handing out aprons or inviting participants to bring their favorite aprons or other utensils from home can be a fun way to personalize the time together.

Another important point to consider when preparing to bake bread together is to identify who will be participating. Will this be a youth group or young adult activity? If so, the young people can be active in shopping and invited into leadership when it comes to cooking and conversing. If younger children are involved, then age-appropriate activities, discussion topics, and kitchen instructions—for instance, not to add the flour too fast to avoid a flour explosion—will help the event go smoother. Groups of adults can also enjoy baking together, entering a time to share thoughts about faith and life that they might otherwise not often have a chance to discuss. Having a good sense of who will be participating will help planners make the most of the time when this group comes together to bake bread for worship.

A final tip about preparation is to consider how to make the ingredients and cooking tools available to the group members. It can be helpful for leaders to lay out the ingredients, along with the appropriate measuring devices for each ingredient, in advance, so that everyone can easily access them when it comes time to start mixing. On the other hand, a leader might simply point people in the right direction when the time comes. Either way, just as the ovens are preheated before the baking begins, a pinch of forethought about how folks will find their ingredients and utensils will support the experience.

Gathering

It is good and customary to start a church gathering with prayer. But why? Like Holy Communion, prayer is a mysterious and multifaceted part of Christian life. Even so, amid the many mysteries of prayer, there are concrete things we can say about what prayer is and what it does. Praying as a community tells us that we are not alone: we are sharing time, space, and experience with other unique and beloved children of God, connected through the love of Christ, who said, "For where two or three are gathered in my name, I am there among them."[15] Praying gives us the chance to thank God, once again, that the Holy Spirit has brought us together for goodness and mutual blessing.

Prayer also names our relationship with the food that the group is about to prepare for the wider community. In one way, prayer sends us backward to consider our connections to the land that the ingredients came from and the people who helped get these ingredients into our lives. In another way, prayer sends us forward to consider those participating in the bread baking, those dear people who will receive this bread in Holy Communion, and all who hunger for God's grace near and far.

We start our bread baking with prayer, because it asks the Holy Spirit to be among us in our time together, grounds us in the reality that our lives happen in fellowship with God and creation, and lets us know that this humble act of service begins in God's love and will share that love with others. Whether a group uses the prayer at the beginning of this chapter or another one that speaks to the

15 Matt 18:20.

community's situation, starting the event with prayer reminds us that—to paraphrase Psalm 31:15—our times are in God's hand.

After the prayer, a leader might welcome the group by saying hello, facilitating introductions, and letting everyone know the plan for the session. Some possible starting questions include: What is a favorite memory about a meal you have had? What memories come to mind when you think about food and church? What seems interesting about baking Communion bread together like this? What kinds of bread have been served at Communion in your churches (wafers, pita, etc.)? Open-ended topics like these give people a chance to get to know one another, feel comfortable in a potentially new setting, and move from introduction to conversation at their own pace. Just as Holy Communion unites people as the body of Christ by bringing them together around the body of Christ, gathering to make Communion bread can include the thoughtful tending of how individuals become a community through faith in God and loving service to others.

Mixing, Baking, and Talking

Hands washed. Aprons on. Ingredients ready. This is the time to get cooking!

While participants focus on mixing ingredients according to the recipe, social mixing is also a key ingredient to the experience of baking Communion bread together. With other times for more structured conversation possible before and after this section, the time for making the dough can be a delightfully free-flowing patter of observations about the recipe, remembering past kitchen adventures (or misadventures), sharing life updates, or quiet concentration. Experienced bakers can share tips with people newer to baking. One or more leaders can buzz around the space, providing steady guidance as needed.

As each recipe indicates, the mixing concludes when the dough is spread by hand or rolling pin into imperfect circles about a quarter-inch thick. Now resting on baking trays that have either been greased or covered in parchment paper, the doughy loaves are brushed with oil. Finally, the sign of a cross is gently made with a knife or spatula edge in the center of each loaf. The cross, of course, visually reminds us of Christ's dying and rising for us, his life given for us and presented to us in this meal.

With the bread in the oven for its first amount of time, the group can come back together for conversation. Inspiring Bible studies can be prepared based on passages like John 6, which includes both Jesus feeding the multitudes on the shore of the Sea of Galilee and his teaching about bread from heaven, in which he said, "I am the bread of life. Whoever comes to me will never be hungry, and whoever believes in me will never be thirsty."[16]

Leaders do not need to be intimidated by the idea of preparing a Bible study. Leading a meaningful Bible study can be as simple as reading a paragraph and inviting people to share something they noticed or wondered about in the passage. They might also be invited to say how Christ's good news spoke to them in the passage. However it happens, the group is invited to ponder how their bread baking is a way of personally living into the story and blessings of Jesus Christ; after all, the New Testament is a meal that they are intimately part of. In this way, the bread bakers become evangelists, too. They are sharing the story and experience of Christ's good news with others in word, deed, and food.

The Cross and Conversation

Just past the midpoint of each recipe's cooking time, the loaves are removed from the oven. Applying a second light layer of oil helps the crust stay firm yet moist. Also at this time, the lines of the cross are deepened and re-emphasized with a knife blade or spatula edge. On a practical level, the dough will have expanded a bit, which fades the original sign of the cross. Theologically, boldly marking a cross on the bread just before it will be finished connects Christ's assurance

16 John 6:35.

of "This is my body" with the bread the congregation will receive in worship.

Of course, any bread used in the sacrament shares this promise. But those who are baking the bread and marking it with the cross will be invited into the devotional practice of picturing the people who will personally receive this gift of grace through these loaves. What friend comes to mind as one carrying heavy burdens and needing Christ's rest? What broken relationships will be brought to Christ's table in the lives of those seeking reconciliation in this meal? What new face might meet Christ for the first time through this bread of blessing?

In the few minutes of waiting for the bread to finish baking, these and other questions can be considered. Or, to keep things simple, a group might discuss what this time together has meant for them in the moment. Maybe someone experienced a new surprise or wonderment while connecting the work of their hands with the gift of Christ's body. This is also a good time to imagine who in the community might enjoy baking the Communion bread next time. If the youth took the lead this time, then maybe a senior group or family ministry leaders might give it a try next. A worship team might bake bread together as part of their reflection on wider aspects of their shared work of planning worship. Children preparing for First Communion will love knowing that they made such a great contribution to the whole church . . . and will enjoy the chance to sample their work ahead of time!

Preparing for Worship, Cleaning, and Sending

Each of these recipes yields two loaves that can be eaten fresh, stored in a refrigerator for a couple days, or frozen in wrap or other containers for a longer time. As is typical of Jesus's ministry with food, they are easily multiplied.[17] Leftover ingredients can be stored

17 See, Matt 14:13–21, 15:32–39; Mark 6:31–44, 8:1–9; Luke 9:12–17; John 6:1–14.

for the next time, and people will likely want to have a next time. There is no need to bless the bread or say a prayer over it, as that will happen in worship. But if enough bread has been made that participants can share a loaf for the sake of fellowship and quality control, then that is indeed something worth savoring, giving thanks for, and enjoying.

Because the group was only making one item (bread), cleaning up from this activity will usually not take very long. Even so, it is good to imagine beforehand how to finish the work of doing the dishes, wiping tables, and putting things away. As we will discuss in other chapters, many congregations have discovered that doing the dishes together is a highlight of the event, because of the extra time for conversation, service, and laughter that cleanup times allow.

Either before or after the cleanup crew gets going, the session ends with time for final reflections and a prayer. Among other ways to end in prayer, the Lord's Prayer (also called the Our Father) provides a beautiful conclusion. Like Holy Communion itself, these words that Jesus gave his followers in Matthew 6 and Luke 11 connect our hearts to both God our creator and the daily bread that sustains life. While the meaning of "daily bread" will be discussed further in chapter 4, the bread-baking participants might be invited to ponder for themselves how the bread of the Eucharist informs the way we think about all that we need for daily life.

COMMUNION CONCLUSIONS

Concluding this chapter reminds us that the sacrament of Jesus's Last Supper is more about new beginnings than it is about endings. For instance, although this meal was given as Jesus's last before his crucifixion, it gave his followers a fresh start after he rose from the dead and sent them out to tell the good news. Although Communion often happens near the end of a worship service, it sends the invigorated congregation out with grace and reconciliation with the words of dismissal that many communities use: "Go in peace. Serve the Lord. Thanks be to God!"[18] And although baking Communion bread is an important but relatively quick task that usually takes no more than an hour, the participants will be looking forward to sharing Eucharist together, to serving their community with this grace-filled food, and to future opportunities to be united in faith, service, and fellowship.

The New Testament is a meal. The food itself proclaims the good news of Jesus Christ, feeds us with God's abundance, and brings us together as the gathered body of Christ.

CONVERSATION AROUND THE TABLE

1. What does Holy Communion mean to you?
2. Share a memorable Communion experience. What made it significant for you?
3. How is the good news of Christ's death, resurrection, and living presence being preached, received, and shared?
4. Imagine a visitor's experience at your church, from the time they enter the church grounds to the time they depart. What would they experience? Hear? Receive?
5. Reflect on your congregation's Communion practices, liturgy, and elements. How are each of the following communicated:
    a. Welcome and belonging
    b. Christ's love for all people
    c. Christian unity as the body of Christ
    d. Care for individual needs (accessibility, food needs, etc.)
    e. Care for creation

---

18 For instance, Inter-Lutheran Commission on Worship, *Lutheran Book of Worship*, 74.

CHAPTER 3

Community Meals

PRAYER

Sustaining Lord,
You shared fish with your friends by the shore,
That they might eat and be restored.
Gather us around holy tables,
So that we, too, may offer what we are able.
Transfigured by your presence and your food,
To share the joy that comes from you.
Amen.

INTRODUCTION: COME AND EAT

Jesus loved to eat with his friends. In the Gospel of John, Jesus's third resurrection appearance took place on the seashore. His friends had fished all night without catching anything, until Jesus told them to cast their nets over the other side. With nets suddenly heavy from the abundance of fish, they recognized Jesus and brought their catch ashore. Unable to wait even that long, Simon Peter jumped out of the boat and swam to meet Jesus on the beach. Their reunion started with an invitation to share breakfast together.

> When [the disciples] had gone ashore, they saw a charcoal fire there, with fish on it, and bread. Jesus said to them, "Bring some of the fish that you have just caught." So Simon Peter went aboard and hauled the net ashore, full of large fish, a hundred fifty-three of them; and though there were so many, the net was not torn. Jesus said to them, "Come and have breakfast." Now none of the disciples dared to ask him, "Who are you?" because they knew it was the Lord. Jesus came and took the bread and gave it to them, and did the same with the fish.[1]

Can you imagine a more welcoming experience than being invited to have breakfast on the beach with Jesus? "Come and have breakfast."

As Pastor Ángel Marrero once noted in an Easter season sermon, tasty fish seems to have been the risen Christ's favorite meal.[2] He ate it multiple times with his friends, including for dinner on the first Easter. Thinking he was a ghost, Jesus's friends were shocked to see him. In response, Jesus asked "Have you anything here to eat?" They gave him a piece of fish, which he took and ate in front of them.[3] Still amazed, the disciples knew he was indeed the risen Christ.

Meals with Jesus are places where grief meets joy, where doubt mingles with belief, and where food sustains the embodied life, power, and promises of God in Christ. Gathered around a meal, Jesus and his followers partook in tangible, nourishing experiences, much like we do when we eat together both within and outside of worship, gathered around Communion rails and tables of fellowship in our own contexts.

The previous chapter explored how theology is expressed in the Eucharist. In this chapter, we will explore the many ways that God meets us in meals that do not include celebration of the Eucharist.

---

1 John 21:9–13.

2 Pastor Ángel Marrero, shared with permission. Pastor Marrero now serves Iglesia Luterana Santísima Trinidad (Holy Trinity Lutheran Church) in Puerto Rico.

3 Luke 24:36–43.

This chapter lifts up the holiness of eating together anywhere and at any time, whether in a private home, a church fellowship hall, a place of work, or outdoors.

ORDINARY FOOD BECOMES A HOLY MEAL

Jesus regularly ministered with, through, and around food. In another scene beside the Sea of Galilee, Jesus had been healing the sick and a large crowd kept following him. Wondering how to feed such a multitude, the disciple Andrew said,

> "There is a boy here who has five barley loaves and two fish. But what are they among so many people?" Jesus said, "Make the people sit down." Now there was a great deal of grass in the place; so they sat down, about five thousand in all. Then Jesus took the loaves, and when he had given thanks, he distributed them to those who were seated; so also the fish, as much as they wanted.[4]

Here again we see Jesus nourishing those who were following him (including multitudes of people he probably had not met before), bringing people together, feeding them, and sharing God's abundance with people who hungered in body and soul.

Intriguingly, the meal in John 6 began with a meager offering of five loaves and two fishes provided by a single boy, showing us that God loves, values, and uses our humble offerings. Whatever we happen to have can be used to do amazing things, such as providing a feast for hungry crowds. The boy gave what he had, and from that offering flowed sustenance that was enough for all.

What humble loaves and fish do you bring to share with God and your community? Some people love to cook or provide assistance behind the scenes, while others love to be out front serving and showing hospitality. Some people are great with ideas, funding,

---

4 John 6:9–11.

fundraising, organizing, and planning a meal. Without realizing it themselves, some might be the kinds of people whom others rely on to give a quick smile, start a welcoming conversation, or share a much-needed hug or handshake. Some outgoing folks love to invite, knock on doors, make phone calls, send evites, and tell strangers about upcoming events. For others, taking part in an event with a lot of new people that might feel noisy and disorienting is not their idea of a good time. For them, simply showing up is a way to share the gifts they bring as a person and beloved child of God. In that way, the informal invitation to "just bring yourself" can be more than a cliché: it's an affirmation of each person's worth and a reminder that God uses our humble offerings. God works through our simplest gifts and regular selves to create transformative, nourishing life. We experience this in the Eucharist as the body of Christ, and we experience this in meals we share as members of a gathered community.

The many regular meals that Jesus shared communicate the truth of the Eucharist. His care for feeding people and sharing fellowship at meals manifested the blessing of communities made whole by the love and grace of God and symbolized the abundance that God daily gives creation. Expressing the Eastern Orthodox connections between Eucharist, food, and God's love for the world, Alexander Schmemann wrote, "In the Bible the food that people eat, the world of which they must partake in order to live, is given to them by God, and it is given as *communion with God*."[5] Similarly, in the experience of many African American worshipping communities, the tradition of communal Sunday dinners "has deep biblical as well as social and cultural meaning. It goes back to the early days of the church, back to slavery. . . . It has to do with communion. Communion was a meal, a feast of love."[6]

Community meals share the reality of heavenly love one stomach at a time, proclaim the message of Christ's love in word, deed, and flavor, and cast a vision for how to live into this love every day.

---

5 Schmemann, 21. Amended for inclusive language; italics in original.

6 Miller, *Soul Food*, 60.

Liturgical scholar Gordon Lathrop has shown how this blended concern for social meal practices and theological beliefs about God's love has been tied together since Christianity's earliest years. For early Christians, "sharing food was then one of the authentic ways of remembering Jesus and continuing his eschatological proclamation."[7] In this way, meals have long been part of Christians' experiences of and expectations for the kingdom of God.

Perhaps nothing expresses this connection between Holy Communion and our regular mealtimes quite as clearly as when Jesus taught his disciples to pray for their daily bread. Receiving our daily bread means being fed with God's word, being united with Christ, who called himself the bread of life,[8] and sharing the goodness of earth's food and drink with the people around us. While the next chapter will further discuss the importance of daily bread, the rest of this chapter describes how the fellowship and nourishment of community meals grow directly out of the grace-filled experiences of Holy Communion and the activity of the Holy Spirit. The risen Christ himself was pleased to share a fresh meal of fish and bread with his friends, as he urged them to "come and have breakfast." Breaking bread with Jesus and each other remains among the most sustaining things we get to do in life.

EATING TOGETHER IN COMMUNITY

In her study of how common biblical subjects like food can enliven contemporary preaching and worship, Gail Ramshaw wrote, "The eucharistic liturgy is based upon the claims that food from God brings life to the community and that the life of our community is food from God."[9] This section's focus on community meals builds upon the tangible, edible, personal, and social side of God's grace for

7 Lathrop, *Four Gospels on Sunday*, 41.

8 John 6:35, 48, 51.

9 Ramshaw, *Treasures Old and New*, 189.

us. It is grounded in the eucharistic meal we regularly experience. Shared meals are a time when mundane practices of food and eating literally serve us with divine favor and flavor. Paying attention to how we eat can reveal the presence and intention of God, while also expressing the deepest values of a community.

The early Christian community shared experiences of Jesus feeding multitudes, extending hospitality, revealing Godself through meals, and eating with all kinds of people. In Acts 2, we hear the story of the new community of believers that arose after the Holy Spirit filled the apostles on Pentecost: "All who believed were together and had all things in common; they would sell their possessions and goods and distribute the proceeds to all, as any had need. Day by day, as they spent much time together in the temple, they broke bread at home and ate their food with glad and generous hearts, praising God and having the goodwill of all the people."[10] The early church gathered around food, generosity, and prayer. They came from a variety of backgrounds, and probably a variety of favorite local foods, to share meals and build a common life together.

As ideal as this might sound, the book of Acts also describes times when the goodwill of the community broke down and challenges of division and discord needed to be overcome. Acts 5 tells about people who did not share, chapter 6 starts with the confession that not everyone was receiving food equally, and chapter 15 ends with Paul and Barnabas going different ways due to their disagreements. An amazing thing about the book of Acts, however, is its story of how the Holy Spirit continued to create life and community despite less-than-ideal, all-too-real complications. The blessed fellowship of Jesus Christ does not avoid sin but does its redeeming and reconciling work precisely amid broken communities and in challenging times.

Indeed, eating together builds new awareness for how people live, lets us learn the hungers of those around us, dispels loneliness, gives and receives hospitality, introduces us to new friends, invites good times together, and creates space to work through disagreements

---

10 Acts 2:44–47.

and engage in hard conversations. While these benefits might sound good on their own, they also show belief in a God who fights against fear, injustice, greed, and sin. We are not stuck in our messes but are invited in Christ to come back to the table again and again. As eco-theologian Jennifer Ayres has put it, contemporary evils of hyperindividualization, isolation, and loneliness are "fundamentally theological and ecological problems."[11] When we come together as a community and hold space for what is real, we are practicing a form of communal repentance, a turning away from the brokenness that engulfs humanity and a turning toward God and God's gracious will for all of creation.

In his book *Food and Faith*, Norman Wirzba shared how community meals can reflect both a Trinitarian appreciation for unity amid diversity and a restoration of the relationship between God and people.

> Though it is possible to describe food and eating in countless ways, from a Christian point of view what food is and why eating matters are best understood in terms of God's own Trinitarian life of gift and sacrifice, hospitality and communion, care and celebration. Trinitarian theology asserts that all reality is communion—the giving and receiving of gifts—because it has its source and sustenance in the eternal Triune love described by theologians as *perichoresis*, a making room within oneself for another to be. This means that nothing in creation exists by itself, in terms of itself, or for itself.[12]

Living and eating together in community develops a relational worldview, in which individuals belong to caring communities that exist not for themselves but for each person in the group.

Making room for another to be who God created them to be—living into that fancy word *perichoresis*, or interrelationship—reconnects

---

11 Ayres, *Inhabitance*, 40.

12 Wirzba, xii.

us with neighbors and creation, both local and global. It shows us how much we truly belong to others and how others are part of who we are. This connectedness then becomes incredibly down to earth when we think about the people involved in producing our food, transporting it, selling and preparing it, cooking it, and sharing it. While we will consider themes of food production and food vocations in more detail in chapter 5, it is helpful when thinking about community meals to see how deeply we are connected and what these relationships say about who God is. Understanding our connection in community as a characteristic of the triune God's own self also invites us to consider how challenges can be faced in productive ways amid our diversities and complexities. There is so much that can happen in a community meal, if we just set the table and show up with what we have to offer.

REAL-LIFE RESOURCES: MANY WAYS TO GATHER

The church potluck is among the most recognized and well-known ways a congregation eats together. People come hungry, often bearing a dish to share, and place their offering on a long table. Folks walk the line of food with their plate in hand, depositing small portions until their plates overflow with bits and tastes from kitchens all around the area. People sit down with friends and neighbors, maybe meeting a new friend during a conversation over plates of food. Indeed, the church potluck is a beautiful image of the body of Christ, gathered to share of themselves for the good of all. When we speak of community meals, it is good to envision typical images of church potlucks, picnics, or dinners. At the same time, it will also be important to challenge ourselves to reflect a little more deeply on these traditional practices, so that we expand our ideas of how communion with God and each other can be shared through a variety of meals, thus creating space for the life and renewal that can come from such experiences.

With so many ways to partake in rich and holy connections over food, the following examples offer a variety of suggestions that might fit various situations. To return to the church potluck image, each style of community meal that is shared here is like a separate dish on the long potluck serving table. These are but a few ideas of how a community might plan and partake in meals together. As in a real potluck, feel free to sample, skip, or come back for second helpings!

Potlucks

The church potluck resonates with stories of early Christians gathering around food being shared with everyone. The word itself is derived from the sixteenth-century English phrase "luck of the pot" to describe a meal thrown together for guests. Indeed, part of the fun of a potluck is finding out which new or favorite dishes might make an appearance.

In North America, Sunday meals have been an important part of church fellowship across cultures. In his book *Soul Food*, Adrian Miller coined the clever phrase "the integration of church and plate" to describe the centrality of Sunday church meals for African Americans in the rural South.[13] Similarly, while teaching seminary students about the experience of people living on both sides of the Texas-Mexico border, theologian Jay Alanís brings the class participants to a *tamalada*, a party for making tamales for a community meal. In addition to the joy of cooking and then eating together, Dr. Alanís has noted a sacramental dimension: "*La tamalada* is eucharistic!"[14] Whether it's the lutefisk of Scandinavian American traditions or pho from Southeast Asia, a wide range of peoples and cultures within a community can be well represented in the truly global variety of favorite dishes that might appear in a potluck.

These shared meals beautifully enrich a congregation's life together. While a community might have its favorite ways to organize

---

13 Miller, 49–50.

14 Rev. Dr. Javier Alanís, email correspondence with authors, February 25, 2021.

its meals, the following questions invite reflection on ways to shift practices so that a potluck can expand opportunities for inclusion and connection.

1. Who is invited to the potluck? How do people learn about it?
2. How is food provided? Are people welcome to attend even if they do not have a dish to share? Is there enough food available to make a satisfying meal?
3. How are individuals invited to bring their full selves to the meal? Consider ethnicity and culture; food allergies, sensitivities, and preferences; disordered eating; children; partner status; and various abilities, disabilities, mobility needs, etc.
4. How is the potluck arranged? Does the logistic setup and access to the meal include or exclude?
5. How is conversation encouraged? Do people sit with the same people each time? How can there be a low-risk way to courageously enter a conversation or dining group?
6. Are there any people who only attend the potluck and not the worship service or vice versa? Why is this?
7. Is the potluck meal connected to the worship experience, or do they exist independently? How can these experiences become more interconnected?
8. What is being preached in the worship service and what is being practiced at the potluck? Are the theologies that are communicated aligned, or disjointed?

Paying attention to questions like these will help a community connect its meals and social times even more directly to the good news message that is shared in worship. Additionally, it is always fair to consider if the message being preached in a sermon is reflected in the meal practices that follow worship, however that meal may be structured.

The spirit and style of potluck meals can enrich other times that people eat together, too. For instance, work and school are two settings that often feature people bringing lunches from home and eating with other people in a cafeteria or break room. Taking care to include everyone, a group can set a date for a workplace or school potluck and create a sign-up sheet. The list of items to bring might include home specialties like pierogies or chocolate chip cookies, or simple staples like a bagged salad or carrots. If young people are involved, fun items like candy or snacks could be included (in moderation!). People who have not signed up, of course, can still be welcome to bring their lunch and hang out. The guidelines can be stated clearly: everyone is welcome, bring what you can, eat what you want.

The food itself can serve as a conversation starter. What are we eating? Where did it come from? What memories do you have of food like this? In such settings, the practice of eating together and thinking about one another can be bonding and meaningful. Potlucks in unexpected places like school cafeterias and break rooms can lead to great conversation and laughter as the focus shifts away from the normal routines of the day and creates new opportunities for storytelling and camaraderie. If there are leftovers, the meal might even have the ripple effect of making plates to pass along to other coworkers and classmates.

In planning for such an event, consider the hospitality inherent in preparing the space for the group, whether that includes having highchairs and small plates available for young children or wide aisles to accommodate assisted mobility devices. Notice who is eating and who could use some assistance. Would someone appreciate their baby being held so they can eat unencumbered? Could it benefit someone to have their plate carried for them through the line so that their food doesn't spill? Does placing utensils and napkins on tables, rather than on potluck lines, create more ease for folks going through the line?

At a potluck, folks come with what they have, bringing a simple offering that is magnified into abundance by the gathered community, just as the young boy's meager bread and fish were transformed into an abundant feast by the seashore. By thinking ahead about how to be truly welcoming and affirming that no offering is too small (including the significant act of bringing oneself), our potlucks become extensions of the Communion table, at which all are fed, nourished, and connected.

Friday Night Meatballs

Another model for a community meal that can take place in church or in a home is something like Friday Night Meatballs. Naturally, this meal can happen any day or time of the week (for instance, after church on a Sunday), but the original idea came from an article by Sarah Grey, who wrote about a new way of sharing food and building community.[15] This is an especially effective model for people with limited time, energy, or space for hosting.

The basic idea is to provide a simple place to gather, an easy main dish that can become a starting point for other meal contributions, and an open invitation that will bring together people who did not know each other before. The space can be a dining room, church meeting room, backyard patio, basement, or even a swept-out garage. Seating can be borrowed and eclectic. Tables can be sturdy furniture or folding fixtures that are set out just for the night. A warm ambiance might be enhanced by (safely) using candles, twinkle lights, or lamps set throughout the room. Open invitations could be extended through social media or in print, giving people the chance to claim a seat at the table via cloud-based sign-up list, texted RSVP, or a verbal yes.

The meals should be as simple as the idea. As the name of this section suggests, one option can be to prepare a large pot of spaghetti,

---

15 Sarah Grey, "Friday night Meatballs: How to Change Your Life with Pasta," *Serious Eats* (blog), *Dotdash Meredith*, https://www.seriouseats.com/simpler-entertaining-friday-night-dinners-end-loneliness-how-to-build-community-after-having-kids.

warm marinara sauce, and a tray of steamy meatballs (or vegetables). Those who accept the invitation could be invited to bring whatever they like or whatever they have on hand: salads, breads, beverages, desserts. In this way, each meal can come together like the people who have gathered: random, a little bit awkward, and deeply nourishing. A card game might follow the meal, or a walk to a neighborhood playground, or perhaps a small outdoor fire around which to huddle and tell stories. No matter how the evening progresses, each Friday Night Meatballs event develops its own flavor and enriches those who have bravely gathered in this way.

Bringing together small groups of various people from different aspects of life—work, church, family, friends, neighbors—invites new conversations, connections, and engagement. Each night offers the opportunity to become its own transformative experience, forged by the food and conversation, welcoming people into life-giving connection. The model of Friday Night Meatballs is a dinner party of the simplest variety, where the prep and planning are minimal, yet the power of eating a good meal together connects, nourishes, and unites those who attend.

While experiences like these can bring joy and build community, it is also important to have hard conversations and serious reflection about what messages are being communicated through both the gathering and the food. Just as we can do when planning for church potlucks, we can consider: Who has been invited or left out, and why? How can hospitality be expanded? What gets in the way of sharing the invitation and the experience? Are we embodying our own theology as we structure and facilitate meals in community?

On a more practical level, issues of dietary restrictions, eating disorders, or basic food preferences are worth considering. In a setting where contact with wheat or nuts, for example, can cause painful or potentially fatal reactions, extreme care must be taken so those with allergies or specific dietary needs are not isolated. Equally important is the language used to describe eating and drinking, as these topics can be harmful to individuals who experience disordered thinking about food or who live with various addictions. How can we communicate about meals and meal-oriented gatherings from a perspective of grace, inclusion, and acceptance for all people? Questions like these will also be addressed in chapter 6, as we consider what hospitality looks like for a large group meal. Here, these questions are relevant for a smaller group meal where people might feel uncomfortable in a more intimate, and therefore more potentially embarrassing, setting. For that reason, give yourself time and grace to imagine what a welcoming, invitational experience might feel like from the perspective of guests and newcomers who will come to the table with varied lived experiences and current needs. As you reflect, here are three initial things that you can specifically address: ask about guests' dietary needs ahead of time, so that there are no surprises at the table and so there is food everyone can eat; when talking about food and drink, engage language that expresses invitation rather than expectation; and make sure there is a suitable nonalcoholic beverage (in addition to water) available for guests to enjoy.

Friday Night Meatballs is a great place to reflect on these topics, as the model is designed to be low stress, easily replicable, and endlessly adaptable with variations including, for instance: Thursday Night Curry Pot, Meatless Monday Meals, Saturday Night Pizza Bar, and so on. As you engage the considerations from the paragraph above and other decisions around practical matters and logistics, this central question can guide all of your planning: how can you bring your community together in a fun, meaningful, and simple way that will communicate hospitality and create opportunities for connection?

Agape Meals

Different forms of the Agape meal might be great option if you find yourself and your congregation wanting to share a holy meal together but do not have a church leader to preside over a service of Holy Communion and the eucharistic elements of bread and wine. "The Love Feast, or Agape Meal, is a Christian fellowship meal recalling the meals Jesus shared with disciples during his ministry, expressing the koinonia (community, sharing, fellowship) enjoyed by the family of Christ."[16] It recalls the experiences of the early Christians who met often for fellowship, to revel in their relationship with Jesus, to eat together, and to worship God in praise and awe.

Similar to Dinner Church, which will be the topic of chapter 6, the Agape meal is a meal that is eaten together as part of a worship service. Unlike Dinner Church, it does not center around the Eucharist. Rather, the meal itself is the heart of the service, with a focus on the connection and unity between those who have gathered to worship and break bread together as members of Christ's body, the church.

This practice can be well suited to many different occasions, including special events or holy days of celebration. Although Holy Communion is not celebrated in the Agape meal, participants are still reminded of the sacredness of bread and the deep nourishment of a meal around the communal table. These meals can also provide an especially meaningful way to shift from a congregational meal that is added to the time after worship to bringing everyone together for worship in and through the meal.

The structure can be similar to a potluck, in which all bring an offering to share. It can also work as a meal that is cooked and served communally. In settings in which people are meeting electronically over the internet, the Agape meal can even provide an occasion for nurturing online community and fellowship when distance or other circumstances keep people from meeting in person.

Regardless of the format, the Agape meal uses a liturgy to guide the service and asks participants to prepare for the meal before the start of worship (a sample liturgy appears later in this book as appendix 2). If people are gathered in one room, food should be

---

16 "The Love Feast," Discipleship Ministries, The United Methodist Church, accessed August 2024, https://www.umcdiscipleship.org/book-of-worship/the-love-feast.

either cooked ahead of time ready to serve or potluck-style dishes set out in time for people to get their food in an orderly way before worship starts. In the context of an online Agape meal, each set of participants should have prepared their food and their space before the liturgy begins.

In the Agape meal, physical, emotional, and spiritual needs are met. Participants are anchored in the shared history of the many times Jesus ate with his disciples, before, after, and during his Last Supper. Worshippers are connected as they come together over food and praise, rooted in tradition through familiar words, songs, and liturgies. The Agape meal experience also affirms worshippers in their own bodies, as all five senses are engaged in a meal. In short, eating and praying together in the Agape meal allows worship to become a fully embodied experience, sustaining and fortifying, not just individuals, but the group as a whole. This powerful practice can strengthen and nourish a community that is meeting together in a room or via a shared internet connection, making the Agape meal a versatile and holy practice, no matter the circumstance.

Youth Group Meals

Food can also help deepen the many formative experiences that often happen in youth ministry. If a group is having an overnight retreat or travel event, the youth can be part of planning the meals in advance, buying the groceries, and packing necessary supplies. Taking turns planning, prepping, cooking, serving, and cleaning can build important life skills and provide great opportunities for new interactions to happen. A group shopping trip can include educational moments like picking produce, reading ingredient lists to learn nutritional values, considering dietary restrictions, and comparing prices. Youth participation can also be integrated into existing food ministries that a church might have, like a weekly meal or Lenten soup suppers, with youth, parents, and other church members cooking side by side.

Almost any aspect of youth ministry can be enriched by a little extra reflection about food. Graduations and other milestone moments can be celebrated by preparing special meals and desserts together. Snacks can be considered in advance so that (whether homemade or store bought) they are extra meaningful, and perhaps less defined by the unhealthy options young people often encounter. Along with trips to fast food places or convenience stores, out-of-town trips might also feature stops at restaurants that expand the youths' palates and horizons. Consider the enrichment that trying new flavors or visiting new restaurants can bring to a group! Not only can new-to-them flavors be discovered, but new foods can expand cross-cultural learning and conversations that might otherwise remain unexplored.

Thinking about food with young people can be a great way to honor their growing bodies and minds. The collaboration involved in planning, cooking, eating, and cleaning up after meals provides unique opportunities for youth to interact with each other and learn with the adults around them. A focus on food and eating can be a delightful way to instill values of service, hospitality, self-confidence, and respect in our youth.

Meetings over a Meal

In addition to transforming youth experiences, food can also add flavor to the frequently bland experiences of committee work and other meetings. Putting a meal on the agenda elevates ordinary tasks and changes the atmosphere of a meeting. In the words of Rev. Carrie Baylis of Colorado Springs, "a meeting without a meal should just be an email."[17] Amen to that! With a plate in front of us, aware of the people around us, minds properly focused on the topic at hand, we are inclined to think about things more fully and creatively. Eating together unlocks something authentic within us, prompting deeper

17 Rev. Carrie Baylis, conversation with the authors, February 2019.

connection and meaning, even if we might find ourselves in the refreshingly awkward position of having to wipe sauce off our faces, clean up spills, or pass a dish awkwardly around the table.

Anchoring meetings with meals, whether home cooked or store bought, can bring nourishment, energy, and joy to a typical meeting, allowing for work and conversation to carry greater creativity and vibrancy. When a committee or team eats together, the meeting itself can communicate and serve the goals of the group by making space for fellowship, honest reflection, and authentic connection to God and one another.

You may think that you do not have time to eat together during meetings. With some advance planning, however, a ninety-minute meeting can be both productive and satisfying. Consider a template for the meetings: begin with prayer or devotion, then continue with objectives for the time together. Gathered around family-style plates of food, the discussion can unfold with ideas, updates, challenging topics, and questions for engagement. By the time the team reaches the end of the meal, it is time to home in on the next steps for the group. In this style of meeting, both the structured conversation starters and the informal chats around the table can help participants get to know each other better, give time and opportunity to think differently about the topic, and foster a sense of engagement and common vision.

For example, perhaps you are a member of a committee that could use a boost in connection, productivity, or purpose. Could your time together be more meaningful if you were to gather around food rather than an empty table? How could the abundance of a nourishing, home-cooked meal or savory snack change your work together and, in turn, transform your larger community? How can space for hard, holy conversations be created when your team comes together around food? Just as we are transformed through the experience of the eucharistic meal, so too do we invite transformation when we gather around our own blessedly ordinary tables. Recalling Jesus's warm invitation to share breakfast with him, imagine the surprise of someone being asked with a sincere sense of joy and abundance, "Come, have a committee meeting with me."

REAL-LIFE RESOURCES: RECIPE STRATEGIES FOR COMMUNITY MEALS

Eating together requires nothing special. There is no need to try new recipes or do something fancy. Instead, eating together should be an invitation to come as we are and to host with ease. When we let eating with the community come simply and naturally, it will be the kind of blessedly ordinary event that we want and need more of.

With that sense of warmth in mind, you might then consider recipes that are easy for you to make. What go-to recipes are most energizing for you? What ingredients do you already have on hand? Instead of burdening ourselves with the need to impress, we can be sure that favorite dishes prepared with love can be both very tasty and fun to share. The following suggestions, therefore, are simply meant to provide some starting points for how you might shape a community meal that works for your context. While any of the meals from other chapters in this book could be used for a simple community meal, the following recipes for pasta, meatballs, marinara sauce, and garlic bread are all offered with a Friday Night Meatballs setting in mind.

Perfect Pasta

Pasta of any kind (including rice pasta or pasta made from beans) is a comfort food for good reason. There are many ways to top your pasta, beginning with a simple dressing of melted butter, sprinkled salt, freshly ground black pepper, and a dusting of grated parmesan cheese. You can offer pasta when people are sad and need to be warmed up, or when they are celebrating, problem-solving, and socializing. Offering a salad (perhaps one of the recipes from chapter 5) along with the pasta makes for a satisfying and refreshing meal.

Cooking pasta is simple, and it can be easily enhanced with a few tips. Adding salt to the water as it boils gives the pasta extra flavor and texture. Generally speaking, one pound of pasta, boiled in four to six quarts of water, will need around one tablespoon of kosher salt. But of course, depending on the type of salt you use,[18] the amount of salt you should add will vary. By tasting the water as it warms, you will learn your preference for how much salt to add. The water should taste pleasantly salty, but not harshly salty. Salting pasta water is a forgiving process: if the water gets too salty, ladle some out and add more fresh, unsalted water. Once the water tastes delicious on its own, add whatever kind of pasta you like. Stir well, then set a timer for a minute less than the package recommends. Stir occasionally, and taste the noodles when the timer goes off. When you bite it in half, your pasta should have a faint white line in the middle of the noodle. Reserve two cups of your salty pasta water and drain off the rest. Now you are ready to top the pasta however you like, using your reserved pasta water to create a sauce, thin out a sauce, or add more flavor down the line.

Simple Marinara Sauce

Whether you are planning to host your own version of Friday Night Meatballs or just want to serve big bowls of spaghetti with sauce and garlic bread, a large pot of homemade marinara sauce can be made with little cost and a few hands-on minutes of preparation.

Begin with your garlic: about eight cloves to a full head of garlic for one large pot of sauce. Break apart the cloves, lay them on their

---

18 Kosher salt is the recommended salt throughout this book. Iodized table salt is not recommended, as this brings an experience of saltiness that is not well-suited to cooking. Different brands of kosher salt each have different levels of saltiness, so be sure to taste each recipe as you go to ensure you aren't over, or under, salting your food.

side on your cutting board, and rest the *flat* side of your knife on each clove, giving it a good thump with the heel of your hand. This will crack the garlic skin so that you can easily peel it off and discard it. Once peeled, mince your garlic cloves. Pour olive oil into a large pot until it thinly coats the entire bottom of it. Heat the oil over medium-low heat. When the oil is warm, add your minced garlic. Stir with a wooden spoon and then, depending on the spice preferences of your community, sprinkle in a pinch or two of crushed red pepper flakes. Allow your garlic to completely soften and become fragrant but not brown, stirring often This should take two to three minutes. Garlic burns quickly! Keep an eye on it as it toasts in the olive oil and be sure to move to the next step as the minced garlic is turning golden. If the garlic turns brown at all, it is burned and you'll need to throw out the garlic and olive oil and start over, as there is no recovery from burned garlic.

As the garlic becomes golden, be ready to add three 28 oz. cans of crushed tomatoes to the pot (sliding the pot temporarily off the heat can help minimize the tomato splatter as they are poured in), followed by two 14.5 oz. cans of diced tomatoes. Stir well to combine. Now come more spices: around a tablespoon each of kosher salt[19] and oregano, two teaspoons of dried basil, and several grinds of black pepper. Stir, then taste. The spices will come together more as it simmers, but you want to know where the flavor is headed.

Neither of the following suggestions are necessary, but they can be nice additions: if you have a rind from an old block of parmesan cheese, add it to the pot; or, if you are of drinking age and have an open bottle of red wine, add a few glugs to the pot (the alcohol will evaporate out of the boiling sauce). Either of these options will add a lovely, rich flavor, although the sauce is also delicious without the additions.

---

19 Adding salt is like cutting bangs: you can always add more salt later, but you can't take salt out or put hair back on once the deed has been done. Start with less, taste, and add more as desired.

Allow the contents to come to a very gentle bubble, then stir and reduce the heat to low. The rest of the recipe is hands off, as the sauce can simmer while covered for as little as thirty minutes and as long as five hours with occasional stirring. To make sure it is as delicious as you want, taste the sauce again when it gets close to serving time and add a little salt or spice as needed. If you added a rind from a wedge of parmesan cheese, it may melt entirely, or a chunk of rind may still remain intact in the sauce. If any of the rind remains, you can remove and discard it before serving. You can either ladle the sauce directly onto individual bowls or mix it together with the pasta. Once cooled and chilled, extra sauce will freeze well for your next community meal.

Meatballs

First, the meatballs are optional. If you are trying to reduce your meat consumption, feeding people who do not eat meat, or are on a tight budget, the meatballs can be easily omitted. Should you want to prepare the meatballs, though, feel free to try the following recipe.

Begin with a chopped onion and several minced garlic cloves, which you'll sauté in olive oil over medium heat until they just begin to brown. Remove the pan from heat and allow to cool. Prepare two baking sheets with silicone mats or foil lightly coated with nonstick cooking spray, and set them near a large mixing bowl. Now take two pounds of ground meat—ideally, one pound of beef and one pound of pork—and add them to the mixing bowl. Here you can add your flavors and binders. This is not a precise formula, because the flavoring is flexible and can depend on what you have in your fridge on that day. For starters, you might take a small bowl of breadcrumbs, around half a cup, and soak them in a little over half a cup of milk while adding other ingredients to the meat. Add the following to the large mixing bowl: a small handful of chopped flat-leaf parsley, a few dashes of hot sauce, a few dashes of Worcestershire sauce, half a teaspoon of Dijon mustard, two beaten eggs, around a tablespoon of oregano, two teaspoons of kosher salt, several grinds of black pepper, and a hearty sprinkle of either nutritional yeast or parmesan cheese. Add the sautéed onions and garlic, along with the soaked breadcrumbs, to the bowl. Now use your very clean hands to mix everything together well and let the mixture sit in the fridge for anywhere from thirty minutes to overnight.

When you are ready to bake the meatballs, turn your oven to 350 degrees. Roll the mixture into small balls and lay them in rows on the prepared baking sheets. If the meat mixture is too sticky, wash your hands and leave them a little wet; damp hands will keep the mixture from sticking to you. Each baking tray can have its own rack in the oven, switching spots halfway through the cooking time. The meatballs will bake for a total of twenty to thirty minutes. They will be ready when you see caramelization, or browning, on the outside and an inside that is cooked through but still moist.

Because this recipe is more about preparation than cooking, it can be nice to make a double batch (four pounds of meat total) and freeze half of them for next time. To do this, line up the rolled, uncooked balls on a baking sheet and place them in the freezer for several hours. Once the meatballs are frozen through, move them to a plastic freezer bag or container and keep frozen until needed. At that time, the frozen meatballs can be placed on a baking sheet to defrost in the refrigerator, then baked as directed above.

Crunchy Garlic Bread

There is no need to buy premade garlic bread at the grocery store when you can make your own in moments.[20] Obtain or make a large loaf of Italian or French bread, then slice it in half, lengthwise. For

20 This recipe is Lauri Lisi's go-to method for making garlic bread. It comes out perfectly every time and is everyone's favorite part of an Italian meal at her house.

each loaf of bread, you'll mix together one softened stick of unsalted butter along with half a teaspoon of salt, two teaspoons of oregano, two teaspoons of garlic powder, and one teaspoon of paprika. Spread thickly on each bread half, and place on a baking sheet. Put it into 350-degree oven for ten minutes, then switch the oven to the broiler setting and allow the top to crisp up for two minutes, keeping a close eye on the bread so it does not burn. Remove from oven, cool for a minute, then slice into thick chunks. Two full loaves of garlic bread will serve four to eight people.

CONCLUSION: MEALS NOURISH BODIES AND RELATIONSHIPS

Eating together happens so often in congregations that it can be easily taken for granted as an essential ingredient in forming faith and fostering fellowship. This chapter has therefore sought to enrich community meals by posing questions and offering ideas that might add purpose and flavor to church gatherings for the sake of renewed community life and effective ministries. Remembering all the times that Jesus enjoyed sharing meals with friends and followers, we can continue to live into that vision of God's generosity, love, and joy by being intentional about the ways we gather around food and invite others to know Christ's friendship and warmth. As seen in both the New Testament and our own communities, holy encounters often start with the simplest invitations to eat together. As Jesus said, "Come and have breakfast."

CONVERSATION AROUND THE TABLE

1. Remember or tell a story of a memorable meal.
2. What do you enjoy about a meal eaten in community?
3. What is challenging about a meal eaten in community?

4. How can you imagine bridging some of the challenges you or others might experience in a community meal?
5. Reflect on your faith community. What kind of community meal might you host in this context?
   a. Who are the partners you should reach out to for shared hosting?
   b. How will you extend an invitation?
   c. Consider the theology of your faith community. How will the community meal be representative of your community's theology? What might detract from your community's theology? How can you address these detractions?
   d. Work through all the logistics related to the community meal, considering the previous questions posed throughout this chapter.

CHAPTER 4

Never Leave Hungry

PRAYER

Dearest Jesus, our bread of life,
In your care creation thrives.
And yet so many do not have enough,
Hungry in body, longing for love.
Lead us to tables of compassion and oneness
Where all will be served with your grace and abundance.
Amen.

INTRODUCTION: "I WAS HUNGRY AND YOU GAVE ME FOOD"

During the season of Lent in 1982, the people of Hosanna—a little church set by a cornfield in northwestern Ohio—were seeking new ways to serve their community. Paying particular attention to issues of food and hunger, parishioners noticed that some people ran low on money for groceries near the end of each month and that others, including senior citizens, regularly ate many of their meals alone. This led Hosanna to start a Fourth Tuesday Meal at the church. Members of the congregation took turns preparing a main dish and providing salads and desserts for these monthly dinners. They added a warm, dignified touch by using linen tablecloths, porcelain dishes, and nice silverware rather than disposable items. Donations and ingredients for meals started to appear from out of nowhere so that the meals were not only sustained but also able to flourish with abundant support and energy from the congregation and the wider community.

Church members enjoyed cooking, serving, and doing dishes together. Everyone who came was treated like an honored guest and friend. Money put into the "offering can" at the meals was dedicated entirely to local food ministries. Over time, the congregation started offering senior lunches, Thanksgiving meals, holiday gifts of toiletries and health items, and blood drives that featured homemade desserts for donors. Through these activities, some informal slogans came to describe the spirit of Hosanna and its mission, including "Give blood—eat pie!" and "Never leave hungry."[1]

As identified in chapter 1, these wonderful community meals and inspiring statements like "never leave hungry" both invite us to claim God's abundance for ourselves and challenge us to pay attention to the ways that people are still going hungry today.

This chapter, named after one of Hosanna's unofficial mottos, lifts up the witness of countless communities of faith to inspire and encourage effective ministries of loving service. Readers will consider how one day, one gathering, one worship service, one personal interaction, one food ministry at a time can be positively impacted by asking what it means that no one leaves hungry. Maybe not leaving hungry means clearly and directly delivering words of grace and welcome in worship. Maybe a church might organize its gatherings with faith that sharing food and hospitality will lead them to be the kind of welcoming place they want to be. Or maybe a congregation prays, listens, learns, and acts in such a way that the scary edge of

---

1 These stories have been shared with permission from email correspondence between Nancy Wright, a charter member of Hosanna Lutheran Church, Grand Rapids, Ohio, and the authors (November 16, 2020).

hunger and food insecurity is relieved at least for a moment through a meal. Humble as such things may seem, these daily connections between grace, food, and human needs are at the heart of the Christian gospel.

As we have already tasted and seen, the good news of Jesus Christ goes through real stomachs. As Jesus said about the acts of mercy that characterize life in his kingdom, "I was hungry and you gave me food, I was thirsty and you gave me something to drink." Expanding on this already incredible identification of himself with those who physically hunger and thirst, Jesus went on to say that those being welcomed into the kingdom had not even realized they had been interacting with him by caring for their neighbors. Responding to that surprise, Jesus said, "Truly I tell you, just as you did it to the least of these who are members of my family, you did it to me."[2]

Inspiring ways to serve Jesus and care for neighbors by connecting food and faith already exist in many congregations, including soup kitchens, food pantries, and advocacy for public policies that serve the well-being of those in our communities. This chapter affirms those ministries and offers further support and imagination for how to build on them or start new hunger ministries. Before doing so, however, this chapter will provide historical examples from the Reformation era of the 1500s and other periods of church history to show how Christians have long supported secular public efforts to address issues of hunger and nourishment. Because so many hunger issues are impacted by the economic and social systems around us, people of faith can contribute to the common good by engaging not only as individuals or as church members but in wider aspects of public policy.

The chapter will then provide stories and resources to inspire new food-based ministries or build on existing ones that serve people in body and soul. Far from trying to provide exhaustive examples of all the ways a congregation can serve its community through ministries that address hunger, this chapter aims to invite and empower readers

2 Matt 25:31–46.

into their own ideas for effective service. As Pastor Emily Scott wrote about starting a worshipping community around food and faith in New York City: "The food will be warm, the singing simple, the prayers from the heart. No one will leave hungry."[3] Like the people in Matthew 25 who were surprised to learn that they had served Jesus by caring for those around them, we will continue to experience God's amazing grace as we see Christ in the lives of those around us, sharing from the abundance that God has so richly provided.

DAILY BREAD, PUBLIC POLICY, AND THE LUTHERAN REFORMATION

Readers in the United States today might be surprised to learn that Martin Luther believed that addressing hunger was a job for political leaders and not primarily a responsibility of the church or individual Christians. Reflecting on what it means to pray "Give us this day our daily bread" in the Lord's Prayer,[4] Luther taught people to "expand and extend" their view of how God provides for our physical needs.

> When you say and ask for "daily bread," you ask for everything that is necessary in order to have and enjoy daily bread and, on the contrary, against everything that interferes with enjoying it. You must therefore expand and extend your thoughts to include not just the oven or the flour bin, but also the broad fields and the whole land that produce and provide our daily bread and all kinds of sustenance for us. For if God did not cause grain to grow and did not bless it and preserve it in the field, we could never have a loaf of bread to take from the oven or to set upon the table.[5]

---

3 Scott, *For All Who Hunger*, 38.

4 The Lord's Prayer appears in Matt 6:9–13 and Luke 11:2–4.

5 *BC*, 449–450.

For Luther, daily bread represents all that we need to live. Bread is both a specific example of God's loving care and an expansive metaphor for the many ways that God provides earthly sustenance, including the fertile land from which food comes, the hands that grow and prepare our meals, clean air and water, and the functional social systems that help deliver food to real stomachs.

Expanding minds to think about bread as a fundamental unit of God's providing, Luther went on to connect this prayer for bread with care for the political institutions and social systems that exist in a very fundamental way to feed people. "Indeed," he said, "the greatest need of all is to pray for the civil authorities and the government, for it is chiefly through them that God provides us daily bread and all the comforts of this life."[6] In Luther's theology, food is both a sign of God's love and the basis for political institutions, economic systems, stewardship of creation, and community values.

Similarly convinced about the importance of government as a means of serving God's creation, Luther's colleague Philip Melanchthon taught,

> Just as the Gospel neither abolishes nor disapproves of arithmetic, architecture, or the science and art of medicine, so it neither abolishes nor disapproves of the economic or political order. Indeed, it commands us to recognize that these things are gifts of God which this physical life cannot be without. Moreover, since God does not will that the human race be destroyed, but that the church be gathered in this earthly life, God preserves our physical life by these things: food, drink, marriage, the civil order, and the arts, such as agriculture, architecture, medicine, and physical life.[7]

Observing that each society would have diverse systems of governance that matched their local customs and cultures, the Lutheran

6 *BC*, 450.

7 Melanchthon, *Loci Communes 1543*, 218–219 [amended for inclusive language].

Reformers of the 1500s valued political and social engagement as God-given and God-pleasing ways to serve neighbors.

Although Luther certainly taught that individual Christians should care that their neighbors have enough to eat and should act individually to address that need, he believed even more that dealing with physical needs like hunger and food insecurity was among the political government's main reasons for existing. He wrote, "It would therefore be fitting if the coat of arms of every upright prince were emblazoned with a loaf of bread . . . or if a loaf of bread were stamped on coins, in order to remind both princes and subjects that it is through the princes' [political] office that we enjoy protection and peace and that without them we could neither eat nor preserve the precious gift of bread."[8] For Luther, hunger was a core political issue. Getting food to real stomachs requires social and political structures that support sustainable agricultural practices: clean air and water; fair wages for people who grow, sell, and cook food; honest weights, measures, and prices in the wider economy; and peace and stability within a land and between nations.

Luther and his colleagues had started tackling social issues like food insecurity in their religious reforms already in the early 1520s. In January 1522, the Wittenberg Ordinance proposed a "common chest" that would provide funding for poor relief.[9] Although that ambitious ordinance encountered general resistance for a variety of theological and legal reasons, the following year saw the nearby town of Leisnig pass a law that included the institution of a common chest to address issues of hunger and poverty. Martin Luther approved of that ordinance, wrote a preface for it, and advocated to the Saxon government on the town's behalf.[10]

The common chests of the Reformation era represented what we might now call a joint public-private venture to address social needs. Public taxes and private donations that had previously gone

---

8 *BC*, 450.

9 Lindberg, *Beyond Charity*, 200.

10 Luther, *Luther's Works*, 45:169–76 [hereafter abbreviated *LW*].

to local religious institutions were set aside for the common chest to fund grassroots ministries and social services. In partnership with church members and ministers, city councils were responsible for administering and dispersing funds.

By the end of the 1520s, Luther's colleague Johannes Bugenhagen—the head pastor in Wittenberg—had further refined the common chest by separating the money for church administration from the money for poor relief, adding efficiency and clarity to the funding of social ministries.[11] In his 1528 church order for the city of Braunschweig, Bugenhagen wrote,

> If we want to be Christians, we must prove this with fruit . . . that is, with true good works of faith which are commanded to us earnestly by Christ, namely, that we show interest in the need of our neighbor, as He says, "Thereby all people will know that you are my disciple, if you love one another" [John 13:35]. We should gladly accept every need of body and soul of our brothers, whether they are rich or poor, as much as we are able, to their comfort. However, here we speak only about the need of the poor, who have no money and must, therefore, suffer a variety of need. The rich are particularly obliged to assist them, as Paul diligently commands them to learn in 1 Tim. 6[:17–19]. In addition, all artisans and workers whom God grants good fortune so that they can surely nourish themselves with the work of their hands, are also obliged to help, as Paul also teaches in Eph. 4[:28].[12]

With many biblical passages and socially conscious arguments, Bugenhagen described why an arrangement like this was both politically beneficial and pleasing to God.

---

11 Lindberg, 144: "Bugenhagen's genius was to separate the fund for poor relief (*Armenkasten*) from the fund for schools, pastors' salaries, and the maintenance of the church (*Schatzkasten*)."

12 Bugenhagen, *Selected Writings*, 2:1378.

Not trusting that the townspeople—including wealthy and influential individuals—would voluntarily give these funds, Bugenhagen's ordinance described how money would be gathered through a combination of public taxes, church tithes, and individual donations.[13] The city council would appoint deacons whose task would be to identify those in need, distribute resources, record income and expenses, and give an accounting of the work. Town hospitals and schools would operate under a similar model. In this way, Bugenhagen set forth a system of social support that was built upon the biblical rationale of caring for neighbors and could be effectively implemented. This shows how the food theology of the early Lutheran Reformation successfully connected religious beliefs about God's love and grace with direct action and political processes that addressed hunger and food insecurity.

LONG-STANDING CHRISTIAN COMMITMENTS TO ADDRESSING HUNGER

Naturally, such connections between physical food and spiritual health were not unique to the Lutheran Reformation, either before that time or afterward. Already in the second century, the Christian writer Justin Martyr described how worship flowed from the bread of Communion to care for those in need:

> And the distribution and the partaking of the eucharistized elements is to each, and to those who are absent a portion is sent by the deacons. And those who prosper, and so wish, contribute what each thinks fit; and what is collected is deposited with the [presider], who takes care of the orphans and widows, and those who, on account of sickness or any other cause, are in want, and those who are in bonds, and the strangers who are sojourners

13 Bugenhagen, *Selected Writings*, 2:1390–99.

> among us, and in a word [the presider] is the guardian of all those in need.[14]

Using images similar to Matthew 25, Justin connected the nourishment given by God in Holy Communion with care for those in need, including those who might be ill, traveling, or imprisoned.

Since the time of the early church and across the centuries, many Christians have been remembered for their generosity to those in need. In a time of persecution before Christianity was legal in the Roman Empire, a deacon in Rome named Lawrence was martyred for his protection of the poor. In the 300s, a bishop named Nicholas was famous for acts of generosity to those who were hungry or in danger. St. Nicholas's care for at-risk children and families became part of the images of Santa Claus that are popular today. In medieval Europe, a compassionate princess named Elizabeth of Hungary used her inheritance to establish a hospital for the poor. One well-known story about Elizabeth also tells of how she risked her safety and reputation to deliver bread to the hungry. Stories like these show how the acts of mercy described in Matthew 25 have been valued and enacted among Christians across the generations.

In the Reformation era, many communities other than Lutherans connected their faith with public policies to end hunger. In a tract on the sacrament of Holy Communion, for instance, Martin Luther praised the Bohemian Brethren for their social concern. Predecessors of today's Moravian Church, these Bohemian Brethren were a reform movement that started a century before the Lutheran Reformation through the leadership of Jan Huss. Aware of theological and contextual differences between their communities, Luther nonetheless commended the Brethren's support of the common good in a letter he wrote to them, saying: "you do not let anyone starve."[15] Such was

---

14 Martyr, "First Apology," in Ehrman, *After the New Testament*, 349.

15 *LW*, 36:305.

the vibrant faith of a community that did not want anyone to leave hungry and demonstrated that concern through their actions.

Communities that remained in the Roman Catholic Church also embraced new and innovative programs for social welfare in those years, as Carter Lindberg has shown in his study of the social reforms that took place in 1525 in the city of Ypres (in modern-day Belgium). This "Poor Order of Ypres" aimed to identify those in the community who were truly in need, to organize effective community funding for those in poverty, and to feed, clothe, and educate local youths, including those from disadvantaged homes.[16]

More radical Reformers of the 1500s—sometimes called Anabaptists—criticized Luther and his colleagues for still seeming too attached to the injustices of the status quo and political systems that privileged the wealthy. These passionate Christians aspired to live out the slogan "Communal living would not be hard / If there were not such self-regard" by removing themselves from the compromises and imperfections of the dominant society.[17] While these Reformers sought purer forms of Christian community, Lindberg pointed out the built-in limits of this approach, especially in contrast to the Lutheran way of working through secular and political institutions: "The irony here is that the Anabaptist emphasis upon a visible church [removed from secular society] precluded the development of a social ethic that could legislate welfare; whereas Luther's emphasis upon the hiddenness of the church [within secular society] impelled such a development."[18] Although the Lutheran approach might suggest compromising with or accepting unjust social and economic systems, Lindberg noted the practical benefits that come from engaging political institutions to provide public assistance and to advance meaningful policies.

Because the political side of public assistance and care for the common good has been a controversial issue in the United

16 Lindberg, 202–206.

17 Lindberg, 158.

18 Lindberg, 160.

States—including among Christians—at least since the time of the New Deal of the 1930s,[19] it is worth offering one more example of Reformation support for political solutions to hunger. In one of his most direct economic statements, the tract *On Trade and Usury* (1524), Luther reflected on Deuteronomy 15:11, which says, "Since there will never cease to be some in need on the earth, I therefore command you, 'Open your hand to the poor and needy neighbor in your land.' " In Luther's view, this verse meant that every political unit was responsible for caring for the basic needs of its people.

> God has expressed it plainly in the law, Deuteronomy 15[:11], "The poor will never cease out of your city." Thus, God has committed to every city its own poor. . . . Although I am too small a man to give advice to popes and to all the rulers of the world in this matter—and do not think myself that anything will come of it—nevertheless, people ought to know what the proper and needful course should be; it is the duty of the authorities to consider and to do what is necessary for the best government of the common people who are committed to their care.[20]

Knowing that people in authority can easily hold shifting or self-interested views of what is good for people in order to deny giving aid, Luther further clarified that the Golden Rule—"in everything do to others as you would have them do to you"[21]—should be used as the measure for public assistance as a way to prevent selfish double standards when it comes to caring for those in need.

In more recent times, theologians around the world have similarly stressed the religious importance of providing direct physical assistance to those in need. In a passage considering the meaning of Matthew 25 for Christian faith and living, Peruvian priest and

---

19 See, Ahlstrom, *Religious History of American People*, 921–29; see also, Koester, *Christianity in United States*, 158–62.

20 *LW*, 45:287 [amended for inclusive language].

21 Matt 7:12.

theologian Gustavo Gutiérrez wrote, "Our encounter with the Lord occurs in our encounter with others, especially in the encounter with those whose human features have been disfigured by oppression, despoliation, and alienation and who have 'no beauty, no majesty' but are the things 'from which men turn away their eyes' (Isa. 53:2–3). . . . This is what Christ reveals to us by identifying himself with the poor in the text of Matthew."[22]

In a 1975 address to the leaders of the Ethiopian Evangelical Church Mekane Yesus, Bishop Gudina Tumsa described how the "holistic theology" of his community connected spiritual vitality with care for people's physical lives.

> Western theology has lost the this-worldly dimension of human existence, and holistic theology is an effort to rediscover total human life. Apolitical life is not worthy of existence, uninvolvement is a denial of the goodness of creation and of the reality of incarnation. We are interested not in creating medieval monasteries, in setting up ghettoes (modern monasteries), but in being involved in the complex social life of our people as we find it daily, with full knowledge of our Christian responsibility.
>
> The history of the people of God in the Old Testament starts with the liberation of a group of slaves from oppression. Nothing is more political than this biblical narrative. In our continent, what is prevalent is the basis to define economic policy, economic development, foreign relations—"Politics decides who should die and who should live." African theology should develop a political theology relevant to the African political life. . . . Political theology should grow out of such experiences on the local congregational level.[23]

Recognizing that political life belongs to the belief that Jesus's incarnation brings holiness to all aspects of being human, Gudina Tumsa

22 Gutiérrez, *A Theology of Liberation*, 116.

23 Deressa and Wilson, eds, *Ethiopian Bonhoeffer*, 87.

advocated for public policies that would serve "total human life." Killed in 1979 by the violent Derg regime which then ruled Ethiopia, Bishop Gudina's commitment to holistic theology has left a lasting impact on the Christian church both in that country and around the world.

While readers of this book on food theology might not have expected or wanted these pages to "get political," bread itself is both deeply religious and political. Policies and practices surrounding food production, distribution, storage, sales, service, and safety are major pieces of what all governments spend their time on. Indeed, food is so foundational to governing that the question is not *if* we should think politically about food but rather *how* we will do so.

From that perspective, we can start with the straightforward statement that God wants people to receive daily bread and that Christ's followers also care about people being fed and healthy. The conversations we have about how to best ensure this is happening in our communities can focus on policies and results, remaining open to dialogue and adaptation. While all kinds of policy solutions might be on the table, one clear thing to say from a Christian perspective is that not caring is not a worthy option. To say it positively: Christians care that daily bread reaches real stomachs.

Knowing that many Christian and community groups currently offer effective hunger relief ministries and advocacy programs, readers are encouraged to learn more about the organizations that might be natural partners with their congregation, either locally, through their denomination, or through other national and global organizations.[24] This chapter will continue by sharing a few of the ways that contemporary congregations are sharing the blessings of food with those who hunger in body and soul.

---

24 For more resources on this topic, see (among many others): Bread for the World, accessed May 2024, www.bread.org; "Food for Life Campaign," World Council of Churches, accessed May 2024, https://www.oikoumene.org/programme-activity/food-for-life; and Feeding America, accessed May 2024, https://www.feedingamerica.org. See also, Nessan, *Give Us This Day* and Yackel-Juleen, *Everyone Must Eat*.

REAL-LIFE RESOURCES: EXAMPLES OF MUTUAL RELATIONSHIPS

In both Bugenhagen's community chest in the Reformation era and the inspiring contemporary food ministries at Hosanna described earlier in this chapter, the foundations of effective service were built upon strong relationships with the community, which prioritized getting to know local needs and gaps in services. Without such efforts to listen and learn, congregations can unhelpfully base their work on faulty assumptions about what others need, thereby missing their goals and disrespecting those they mean to serve. It is also possible for Christians to behave as though they, rather than Jesus, are the world's saviors. Such attitudes and approaches can lead to ineffective, unwanted, out-of-touch, and invasive practices, neglecting the God-given dignity of all people. In contrast, taking time to listen and learn what would be most useful to individuals and communities can foster relationships of mutuality, genuine service, and respect.

In *Compelling Knowledge*, Mary Solberg writes there are three steps to engaging with the work that are needed to heal brokenness: first, people must be willing to see what is going on in the world or in their local community and to recognize suffering and brokenness. Second, because much suffering is caused by humans, people must individually and collectively recognize their personal responsibility and comprehend that these experiences have something to do with them. Third, because God is already present and active in places of suffering, people are called as agents of God to join God in places of suffering, to participate in the healing and restoration God is doing in the world. Because of their recognition of the truth of their complicity in creating brokenness, people are then moved to repentance and love as faithful responses to God's grace.[25]

The accompaniment of others can take place when we begin with responding to God's grace. This helps us to be attentive to needs in our community as people who can walk alongside others, rather

25 Solberg, *Compelling Knowledge*.

than as people who are trying to save or rescue them. When we accompany others, the door is opened to mutual relationship with shared power and dignity for all. In a mutual relationship we can contribute to work that is already happening, engage in authentic interaction outside acts of service, and make space for people with diverse perspectives to participate in decision-making. This multiplies opportunities to listen well to needs that exist and to get to know the gifts, joys, struggles, and sorrows in others' lives. Accompanying others is a faithful approach to engaging in the work that is needed to understand and respond to brokenness in our communities, meeting God where God already is.

MINISTRIES OF ACCOMPANIMENT

We see mutual relationships taking place in many congregations engaged in food ministries. One such example is within congregations that support small, local food pantries. While pantries can be managed by a congregation, some church food pantries are managed by the community members they serve. In this latter form of communal engagement, neighbors are empowered to meet their own local needs, instead of a congregation deciding their needs and dictating the terms of operation. This structure helps ensure that the available food and other items are well suited to the community's desires, while building trust and operating in a way that offers dignity for those who are served.

This care for recognizing local need and inviting others to engage freely served as the premise of the "Little Free Pantry" movement, which provides simple and anonymous ways to share food. According to its website,

> Jessica McClard launched the grassroots mini pantry movement in May 2016 in Fayetteville, Arkansas, when she planted the Little Free Pantry Pilot, a wooden box on a post containing food, personal care, and paper items accessible to everyone all

> the time, no questions asked, [hoping that it] would pique local awareness of food insecurity while creating a space for neighbors to help meet neighborhood food needs. . . . By August 2016, the movement was global.[26]

With a Little Free Pantry, the pressure of asking for help or the shame of accepting help is relieved with a quick, anonymous way to secure food items. While being aware of zoning regulations and local cultural traits that might either enhance or hinder the impact of these efforts, this movement invites congregations, community organizations, and individuals to share in leadership and management of the operation.

Another transformative food and fellowship ministry rooted in mutual relationship is the FEAST program at Our Saviour's Lutheran Church in Lincoln, Nebraska, which developed when a correctional center and a congregation partnered with one another to grow mutual relationships and serve the needs of both communities. Each Sunday, incarcerated people, called "partners," are picked up by congregation members and brought to the church, where they attend worship with the opportunity to be joined there by family members and friends. After worship, partners are invited to enjoy a meal together. Congregation members often join in the meal. Partners are sometimes included in planning and preparation of the meal, too, especially during the weeks in which area congregations and Our Saviour's small groups are unable to provide food.[27]

Ministries are always shifting in response to community needs, leadership, and available resources. The FEAST program is a good example of how ministries can shift in response to internal and external changes. As congregational leadership has shifted, FEAST has taken different shapes, alongside changes that have taken place at the Community Correctional Center of Lincoln. While the

---

26 "Who We Are," Little Free Pantry, accessed May 2024, https://www.littlefreepantry.org/what-we-do.

27 Tobi White, email correspondence with the authors, August 28, 2024.

program once included community time with singing, studying, and sharing following lunch, FEAST partners now join the congregation members in whatever the congregation is offering for Christian education immediately following the church service. This includes Bible studies, presentations, and even congregational meetings. This shift in engagement has created even more active participation and an integrated approach to the ministry, which has been warmly received by both communities. Pastor Tobi White notes that, at its best, there has been shared planning and purpose between FEAST partners and leaders, creating options desired and enjoyed by all.

Throughout the changes in the program, efforts have been made to serve both communities well and avoid the pitfalls of the group with more power (the congregation) making all the decisions for a group with less power (the partners). In this model of accompaniment and partnership, deep relationships have been formed and sustained throughout the years. Some FEAST partners have continued to worship at Our Saviour's following their release from the correctional center, a welcome, but certainly not necessary, result of the positive mutual experiences that formed one meal at a time.

At Holy Trinity in Dubuque, Iowa, in addition to the daily food available through a twenty-four-hour accessible pantry in the secured lobby of the building, the congregation hosts quarterly food distribution events where hot breakfast is a highlight. While some volunteers come early to set up the shopping area where individuals and families will select the items they would like, other volunteers work in the kitchen preparing cinnamon rolls and breakfast sandwiches. The food is set out on tables in the sanctuary alongside juice, coffee, and fruit. Visitors are welcome to eat while they wait in pews for their turn to shop. Members of the congregation mill throughout the sanctuary, sitting to talk with folks while sipping on coffee, bringing cinnamon rolls to children, and learning about the people who have come to shop on this particular day. Hospitality is also extended through the shared use of name tags. In this way, visitors can be called by name (if they want) and are not visibly set apart from the volunteers who work the event. Such intentional hospitality, along with visitors' own selection of their grocery items, creates a welcoming experience that honors personal dignity and is enjoyed by both volunteers and visitors alike.

Just as important as offering food and eating together locally is participating in advocacy work. In the Evangelical Lutheran Church of America (ELCA), churchwide efforts include intentional advocacy for hunger in the world through the World Hunger team. The World Hunger team defines "hunger" as any place where needs are not met. Thus, working to meet the needs of more than 820 million hungry people, ELCA World Hunger "reach[es] communities in need. From health clinics to microloans, water wells to animal husbandry, community meals to advocacy,"[28] the World Hunger team raises funds, builds relationships, and connects with communities on the ground to meet the actual needs of people in those communities. While the work is international, there is also a strong domestic orientation that works toward the "prevention and alleviation of hunger" close to home. This work includes paid staff, volunteers, local synods, and congregations who work together to "address poverty, hunger, and related social justice issues."[29] Currently, World Hunger funds twenty thousand grants for domestic churches to start feeding ministries in their communities. This empowers neighbors to address the hungers they see in their own contexts, in their own time. As expressed by Kayla Zopfi, who works with the team on multiple levels, the work of World Hunger "is rooted in the wisdom and experience of local communities."[30]

In addition to its on-the-ground work, World Hunger participates in national and local advocacy, inviting local community members who care about food-related legislation to meet with their nationally elected representatives for guided conversation, questions,

---

28 "ELCA World Hunger," Evangelical Lutheran Church in America, accessed August 2024, www.elca.org/hunger.

29 "Domestic," accessed August 2024, https://www.elca.org/Our-Work/Relief-and-Development/ELCA-World-Hunger/Our-Approach/Domestic.

30 Kayla Zopfi, in discussion with the authors, August 13, 2024.

and advocacy. A meeting between Iowa state senators and Iowans from various parts of the state, for instance, included conversation about concerns involving childhood hunger, lengthy bus rides, food deserts, care for farmers, and experiences with local food pantries.[31] Zopfi and her colleagues use these meetings as opportunities, not only to influence policy, but also to engage young people who care passionately about their communities and the hungers they experience.

The Dwelling in Winston-Salem, North Carolina, understands hunger in the same holistic way, listening to the needs of the community to guide their multifaceted ministries. In addition to regular neighborhood block parties, weekly shower opportunities, and other social events, the community of The Dwelling is anchored in the meals they eat together. "As a mission congregation which intentionally builds community with the housing insecure," the community names the cultivation of belonging as an important part of their mission.[32] That belonging is lived out each week by claiming the waters of baptism and gathering around the table. Here, says lead Pastor Emily Harkins, "outsiders are no more" because everyone has a valued place. The congregation's meals function, then, as an extension of their Communion liturgy, as participants are restored, included, and invited into healing. Chef Joseph Hedrick heads up mealtime at The Dwelling, with the philosophy that "food is medicine."[33] Visitors to The Dwelling "can always count on a high-quality, home-cooked meal every Sunday," with both breakfast and lunch served each week. Harkins says, "when we eat together, we are also healing together,"[34] which extends the proclamation of the gospel from pulpit to table. As bodies and souls are fed simultaneously, The Dwelling's ministry of nourishment and abundance happens in partnership with the

31 Zopfi, discussion.

32 The Dwelling, accessed August 26, 2024, https://www.thedwellingws.org/.

33 Rev. Emily Harkins, conversation with the authors, November 29, 2024.

34 Harkins, conversation.

neighbors they serve, addressing a variety of human hungers and working in mutual relationship for the good of all who gather.

In each of these examples, no single group dominates or exercises inappropriate authority over another. Instead, we see an enactment of the community chest for which Bugenhagen and his reforming colleagues advocated. Restorative, mutual relationships are made, broken systems are acknowledged, and power and dignity can become shared experiences.

Your community might already have a food pantry, advocacy program, mealtime ministry, or other partnership that connects the gospel with real stomachs. That is wonderful! Your experiences and service are important contributions to the community and strong testimonies to God's love for this world. These grassroots ministries are worth celebrating, sharing, and building on. Remembering Hosanna's vision that people "never leave hungry" can invite us to listen ever more deeply to what it means to serve our neighbors in such a way that God's presence is revealed, and everyone is changed for the better in the encounter.

TWO SIMPLE AND DELICIOUS RECIPES FOR LENTILS

The shelves of food pantries across America are lined with dusty bags of flat, oval, mystery beans. A standby at food giveaways, these bags of brown lentils provide a solid nutritional punch with little preparation time. However, many people do not know what to do with these small legumes, thus leaving them to sit (and maybe sit and sit) unused. What follows are two quick ways to cook with lentils. Both require access to a stove and clean water. To meet the needs of those who visit your food pantry who may not have easy access to a stove and clean water, your community may consider preparing several bags of lentils in the simplest way possible (water, heat, olive oil, salt) and invite shoppers to scoop cooked lentils into plastic takeaway containers so that they can eat them plain or add whatever extra ingredients like vegetables, toppings, or hot sauce they may enjoy.

Because they are packed with plant-based protein, fiber, iron, B vitamins, magnesium, zinc, and potassium, lentils can serve as both a great main dish and a tasty side. While there are multiple kinds of lentils, including red, green, brown, orange, and yellow varieties, this section will focus on brown lentils, as these are the variety often found in food pantries. Quick to cook, they hold their shape well and can complement many other ingredients and dishes. A one-pound bag of dried lentils will equal approximately five cups of cooked lentils.

Begin with two and a half cups of dried brown lentils (approximately one pound, although you can easily scale this strategy up or down, as needed). As with all legumes, give the lentils a good rinse before you begin preparations. Once rinsed, add them to a pot along with a little more than twice the amount of water and two teaspoons kosher salt.[35] Bring the pot to a boil, cover, and allow to simmer. Cooking time will be twenty-five to thirty minutes. Be ready to pull from the heat as soon as the lentils have the texture that you and your community enjoy; some people like their lentils a little firmer, while others boil them until they are completely soft. Once you have tasted them and found the texture you like, remove them from the heat and run them under cold water so that they do not continue to cook and get mushy. Once cooled, you might drizzle the lentils with olive oil and sprinkle with salt, then package these ready-to-eat lentils for giveaway or put them in your fridge for use later in the week.

If you are preparing the lentils to eat right away, then you can begin adding ingredients as soon as they have been removed from the heat and given a good rinse with cool water. Below are ideas for a lentil salad and a lentil soup.

---

35 Whether legumes should be salted prior to cooking or only after cooking is debated in the culinary world. Either way can turn out delicious, so pick one method and carry on confidently, tasting as you go to ensure you are neither over nor under salting.

Lentil Salad

Drizzle the cooked and lightly rinsed lentils with about two tablespoons of red wine vinegar and one tablespoon of olive oil. Sprinkle half a teaspoon of salt and mix everything together. The lentils are already delicious at this point, but you can make them into an even more robust dish using anything else you would like to add. Options include:

- Feta cheese, pitted and sliced kalamata olives, halved cherry tomatoes, sliced spinach, chopped cucumbers, along with garlic powder, onion powder, and oregano
- Chopped pickled vegetables, or *giardiniera*, and thinly sliced red onion
- Chunks of cheddar cheese, sliced black olives, sliced sundried tomatoes, destemmed and thinly sliced lacinato kale leaves, along with garlic powder, onion powder, and oregano

Chill the mixture so that all the ingredients come together and the flavors meld. You can eat your lentil salad cold out of the fridge or at room temperature.

Lentil Soup

Prepare the lentils as listed above, but cook them for only twenty minutes, leaving them still a bit crunchy. At the same time that you start preparing the lentils to cook, chop your vegetables. With five cups of cooked lentils (one pound of dried lentils), you'll want one yellow onion, four peeled carrots, four stalks trimmed celery, and four cloves of minced garlic.

Begin with the chopped onion added to hot olive oil in a large soup pot. Stir, sautéing for four minutes, then add the chopped carrots and celery to the pot, along with a bit more olive oil and one teaspoon kosher salt. Stir and sauté for four additional minutes, then add garlic to the hot oil and sauté together for one minute. You can also add a pinch or two of crushed red pepper flakes simultaneously with the garlic and allow that to get a little toasty. Then prepare your soup base by adding stock to the sautéed vegetables (approximately twelve cups of stock for one pound of dried lentils) and bring it all to a simmer. Drizzle the cooked lentils with one tablespoon red wine vinegar, then add the cooked lentils to the soup pot and bring it back to a simmer for ten minutes. Taste and adjust seasoning as desired. This recipe is the basis for other directions you may want to take the lentil soup, or it can be eaten as is!

For a carbohydrate addition, you can prepare rice in a separate pot, then add the cooked rice to the soup pot following the addition of the stock. Preparing the rice in a separate pot will protect the rice from absorbing all the liquid of the soup and help you avoid mushy rice or overly thick soup. Alternatively, diced potatoes are delicious additions to a lentil soup. If you include potatoes, add them in after the garlic and allow everything to sauté together for five more minutes, then cover with stock and bring to a gentle boil until the potatoes are tender. This takes around twenty minutes, depending on the size of the potato pieces.

To serve a thick lentil curry soup, add a tablespoon of curry powder to the pot at the same time as the garlic. Stir well and allow to cook for one minute. Then add one can of unsweetened, full fat coconut milk and one cup of vegetable stock. Stir together well. Add the cooked lentils (and carbohydrates, if using) when the liquid is heated through. Taste and adjust curry, salt, and liquid as needed.

CONCLUSION: PARTICIPATING IN GOD'S LOVE FOR ALL

We are surrounded by hunger. Our food systems are burdened by inequity, injustice, and greed, so that too many people in our world go hungry each day. While we cannot quickly or sufficiently reallocate all food resources to those in need, we can pay attention to the hungers in our community—hungers that exist in body, mind, and spirit—and to the work that many local organizations are doing to meet those hungers. As we boldly pray that all people might have the daily bread they need, so too can we boldly seek to accompany our neighbors. In humility and repentance, we can acknowledge the deep needs that exist, confess our own contributions to that brokenness, and look for where God is already active and calling us to go next. Showing up in such situations leads to mutual transformation, an alignment with the gospel of Jesus Christ that goes through real stomachs and proclaims God's abundant love for all people.

CONVERSATION AROUND THE TABLE

1. Are there hungry people in your neighborhood or community? How do you know?
2. What does your congregation or organization currently do to meet the hunger in your local area? What are other local congregations or organizations doing?
3. Have you ever been a recipient of a food-based ministry? How did it feel?
4. Name a place in your life where you have power and others do not. Name a place in your life where you do not have power and others do. What does good leadership and communication look like in each of these contexts?
5. When do you engage in authentic conversation with people who are different from you or who have different challenges from you?

CHAPTER 5

Fields and Tables

PRAYER

Gardening God,
Your fingerprints cover the land
Valleys, hills, and plains formed by your hand
Landscapes of grace in which we grow
Beloved soil from which we come, to which we go
Guide us each in doing our part
Serving in body, mind, and heart.
Amen.

INTRODUCTION: GOD THE GARDENER

God is a gardener, and humans are creatures the Lord formed from right out of the ground.

According to the creation account in Genesis 2, before there was even a garden of Eden for people to live in, "the LORD God formed man from the dust of the ground, and breathed into his nostrils the breath of life; and the man became a living being."[1] In Hebrew,

1 Gen 2:7.

Adam is a name that means "from the *adamah*," which means soil. Similarly, the Latin language connects humans with *humus*, which is Latin for soil. We are earthlings made of earth; groundlings from the ground. Indeed, Genesis 2 is a story of our *hum*ble yet divine origins, in which the dust of the earth gets filled with the life-giving breath of God to become humanity. We are Spirit-breathed soil, amazing and lovely, and deeply loved by our good creator.

Genesis 2 continues with God setting the first person in a garden in Eden (a name which means "pleasure") to care for and tend the trees and plants springing from the ground. In this beautiful origin story, humans have been made to work in harmony with creation. We are stewards, whose first calling or vocation is the pleasure-filled work of caring for this awe-inspiring planet together.

In this work we are never alone. In addition to living with a loving creator, surrounded by abundant waters, and tending the bountiful plants, the first person gave names to the animals and was then joined by a human companion, whom he later called Eve "because she was the mother of all living."[2] It is worth mentioning that the name Eve is connected not to the Hebrew word for mother but to the word for life.

The story of Adam and Eve in Genesis 3 describes how the original harmony among God, humans, and creation was broken. However, far from being a tragic piece of ancient history about two people who lived a long time ago, this is our story. It describes the very current reality of how all of us find ourselves out of harmony with God, the land, and each other. As much as we might lament this situation, it is the true mixed-up condition that each one of us experiences in life: we have been hurt and we hurt others. As much as we might want to "be like God, knowing good and evil"[3] or just escape this condition altogether, we find ourselves unable to set things right on our own.

The word of God knows this about us. Everything in the Bible that follows Genesis 3 is about God walking with us and working with us to lead us into good paths, not ignoring our fallenness but

---

2 Gen 3:20.

3 Gen 3:5.

coming to us in our weakness. In the Hebrew scriptures that follow this story of Adam and Eve, God's promises to the people of Israel will continuously call them into love of God and neighbors, with prophets, priests, and poets leading them back to lives of honesty, trust, and loving kindness.

In the New Testament, which was a meal of reconciliation before it was a collection of writings, faith in Jesus Christ restores the broken relationships among God, people, and creation that humans cannot mend on their own. The book of Acts describes a restoration of harmony that came through faith in Christ and the presence of the Holy Spirit: "Now the whole group of those who believed were of one heart and soul, and no one claimed private ownership of any possessions, but everything they owned was held in common."[4] God's harmonious salvation reached both the hearts and the daily lives of those first believers, not by ignoring their sinful conditions but by transforming them.

In God's promises to the people of Israel, in the crucified and risen life of Jesus Christ, and in the ongoing presence of the Holy Spirit among us, God the Good Gardener continues to tend the soil of our lives and of this beloved creation. Jesus taught his disciples about God's abiding care for both human relationship and all creation in John 15, as he said, "I am the true vine, and my Father is the vinegrower. . . . I am the vine, you are the branches. Those who abide in me and I in them bear much fruit, because apart from me you can do nothing. . . . My Father is glorified by this, that you bear much fruit and become my disciples."[5] Through this gardening metaphor, Jesus connected God's good work as gardener with what it means to abide in him and follow him. Knowing that we live in a fallen, sinful, and hurting world, Jesus brings us back to the reason we exist in the first place: to know ourselves as beloved creatures who have been blessed to care for this dear creation and for one another.

---

4 Acts 4:32.

5 John 15:1, 5, 8.

VOCATION: SERVING ONE ANOTHER IN DAILY LIFE

If, as Martin Luther wrote, "daily bread" means everything we need for daily life, then each of us participates in helping answer this prayer for one another through the actions we take in daily life. Parents care for children, who grow up learning to care tenderly for themselves and others. Doing an honest job at work allows people to receive goods and services at fair prices that benefit families and communities. Being good neighbors, concerned citizens, and fellow members of this beautiful creation fosters actions that invite life to flourish. These everyday paths of service belong to the Christian life no matter what job or role a person has. We all contribute to the world by sharing life with the people God has put in our lives.

More than a religious calling for the relatively few people who work in church or service professions, the Christian concept of "vocation" describes how every person honors God by caring for others in down-to-earth ways. Introducing a collection of essays that invites teachers and college students to think about how education and personal growth support the common good, Erin VanLaningham has written, "vocation is relational, not only between persons but also between persons and environments on every level, including home, neighborhood, community, workspace, the climate, and the universe. The call to communal well-being, serving others beyond self, means attending to the relationships we have and how our identities emerge through these connections."[6] While the temptation to break God's harmony by putting ourselves first remains no less for us than for Adam and Eve, our deepest selves emerge in the joy of belonging to God with others.

When crowds started asking what they should do to prepare for the coming messiah, John the Baptist spoke to the basic value of serving one another in whatever role they might find themselves in, including potentially controversial or conflicted ones. In a world of limited possessions, John told people to share what they had. In

---

6 VanLaningham, *Called Beyond Our Selves*, 15.

a territory occupied by the Roman military, John told soldiers not to abandon their posts but to practice restraint and justice in their work. In an economic system in which tax collectors could gouge people by charging more than what was owed, John said not to find another job but to simply be honest. As the Gospel of Luke tells us,

> the crowds asked [John], "What then should we do?" In reply he said to them, "Whoever has two coats must share with anyone who has none; and whoever has food must do likewise." Even tax collectors came to be baptized, and they asked him, "Teacher, what should we do?" He said to them, "Collect no more than the amount prescribed for you." Soldiers also asked him, "And we, what should we do?" He said to them, "Do not extort money from anyone by threats or false accusation, and be satisfied with your wages."[7]

John the Baptist's vocational message is simple: everyone can prepare the way for the kingdom of God not by escaping their place in the world but by living into it with integrity, love, and care for their neighbors.

All of us have vocations related to food. We cook and eat. We prepare meals or eat meals prepared by others in homes, restaurants, and workplaces. Some of us might garden or farm; others might harvest, transport, clean, package, cook, or serve food for others to enjoy. Health care providers help food do what it is supposed to in our bodies, as we learn to make nutritious choices about what we eat and drink, chew our food with strong teeth, and process it with the many amazing systems—including the digestive system—that our bodies use. Educators teach young people to develop practical and intellectual skills that will allow current and future generations to thrive. Some people might work in businesses that promote healthy food systems, while others work for public or private agencies that oversee food availability, public safety, and sustainable agricultural

---

7 Luke 3:10–14.

policies. Whatever our various relationships to "daily bread," the land, and each other, food gives us many important and grace-filled roles to live into.

REAL-LIFE RESOURCES: TENDING GOD'S GARDEN TOGETHER

Throughout this book, the statement that "food is doing the theology" has pointed to the ways that God's daily sustenance directly reaches us and nourishes us. This chapter expands on that observation to highlight how food also gives us rich vocations and callings. Whether these vocations are paid jobs or informal identities, the relationships that food creates between us and others can be holy outlets of blessing. Recognizing these callings as truly God-given paths of service and love can help us get past the faulty idea that religious vocations are only for people who do professional church work. Instead, by thinking about vocation as a broad category (and as a "daily bread" category), we affirm the many wonderful ways that food connects us all to profound ways to share God's abundance as followers of Jesus Christ, as caring members of our communities, and as fellow stewards of our common home, the earth.

God is a gardener. Simple as it may sound, our own literal efforts at gardening provide great benefits to individuals, neighborhoods, and the environment. On a personal level, activities like digging, planting, watering, weeding, and watching things grow feel very satisfying! It is hard to have a bad time in a garden. Making salsa, pesto, or salads from lettuce, tomatoes, peppers, and herbs grown in one's own garden not only tastes good but can be a great way to share abundantly with neighbors. Also, because so much of contemporary agricultural practice reduces environmental diversity in favor of "monocropping" (that is, planting only one crop like corn or soybeans on vast stretches of land), local gardens have important roles to play in supporting insects and animals that need diverse plant life to thrive.

Whether by tending decorative flowers, growing herbs and vegetables, planting a pollinator garden, or raising healthy neighborhood trees, simple efforts at gardening can bring both personal satisfaction and meaningful environmental benefits. This is the joy that small children have when they plant a single seed in a cup of soil, water it, and watch it grow. We are all connected to the land, and blessedly so.

Community Gardens

In addition to providing personal enjoyment and supporting healthy ecosystems, some community gardens exist to address specific neighborhood challenges like a lack of affordable fresh produce or a shortage of green space. Alice's Garden in Milwaukee, Wisconsin, for instance, is an urban garden and community center that "provides models of regenerative farming, community cultural development, and economic agricultural enterprises for the global landscape. [Participants] recognize the cultivating, preparing, and preserving of food, and food traditions, as cultural arts to be reclaimed and celebrated fully in urban agriculture."[8] Built on the site of an abandoned freeway project for which historic neighborhoods connected with the Underground Railroad had been demolished, the garden was established in the 1970s; in 2001 it was named after Alice Meade-Taylor, a longtime educator and advocate in Milwaukee.[9]

Venice R. Williams has served as executive director of Alice's Garden since 2014. As an authorized lay minister, Williams also oversees programming for a worshipping community called The Table. Bringing these and other community leadership roles together, Williams and her colleagues connect horticulture, counseling services, entrepreneurial opportunities, educational classes,

---

8 "Alice's Mission," Alice's Garden Urban Farm, accessed June 2024, https://www.alicesgardenmke.com/alice-meade-taylor.

9 "History," accessed June 2024, https://www.alicesgardenmke.com/new-page-1.

religious gatherings, and social events.[10] When a congregation in north Milwaukee closed in 2022, the church chose to give the building to The Table, repurposing the space in ways that honored the congregation's witness, including its longtime support of neighborhood food ministries. In addition to serving as an important hub for bringing people together, the many food-related programs taking place in the former church building caused Williams to reflect how "the other thing that this space reminds us of is the sacredness of food."[11] Indeed, as Williams said in an *Milwaukee Journal Sentinal* article written when the building became the 2022–2023 home of the Milwaukee Winter Farmers Market, "Food and faith cannot be separated for me."[12]

Alice's Garden, The Table, and other neighborhood networks and assets show the impact that can come from listening to grassroots needs and acting locally for the good of those around us. This is true whether we live in urban, suburban, small city, or rural settings. As Dr. Monica Smith has written, "Our shared humanity and obligation to contribute to society are key in realizing vocations that contribute to justice and ultimately dismantle systems of injustice."[13] While this work of tending to our communities can often seem slow and not very flashy, the fruits of these labors can be new relationships, increased equity, and new opportunities for people and communities to thrive.

When Our Saviour's in Lincoln, Nebraska made the decision to begin a community garden, they first engaged in several conversations. They met with a local community garden collective called

---

10 "The Table," accessed June 2024, https://www.alicesgardenmke.com/new-page.

11 Carol Deptolla, "A closed church gives Milwaukee Winter Farmers Market a new home," *Milwaukee Journal Sentinal*, November 11, 2022, https://www.jsonline.com/story/life/food/2022/11/11/milwaukee-winter-farmers-market-the-table-get-new-home-closed-church/69638754007/.

12 Deptolla, "church gives Market home."

13 Smith, "Diversity, Equity, Inclusion, and Justice" in VanLaningham, *Called Beyond Our Selves*, 97.

Community Crops to learn how they operated and what the congregation would need to get started. Then they talked with a local elementary school to learn their joys and challenges, including issues of food scarcity in the neighborhood. Out of those relationships grew a vision for a "teaching garden" that would teach skills and concepts so that neighbors and other community gardeners could learn and grow more food themselves.

The congregation set to work to restore garden beds that were accessible and ready for planting. By taking the time to be in communication with the local organizations already active in the area and to spend time volunteering with those organizations, the congregation built trust and relationships. From there, they were able to listen well and respond to the needs that existed, rather than just fulfill their own hopes or visions.

The garden on the church grounds now supplies vegetables for the lunches they serve, and they also use the produce to host canning sessions with the congregation, making salsa, spaghetti sauce, and preserved carrots. The jars have been offered as in-kind donations to raise money for their sister parish in Tanzania at their Tanzanian Brunch and Auction.[14]

If a congregation wants to start a community garden, leaders should consider what the neighborhood needs, where the garden will be located, how to cultivate healthy soil, whether there is the need to protect plants from wildlife, what specific skills may need to be taught and modeled, who will tend it during the growing season and beyond, and who will be responsible for various aspects of the garden. Some congregations follow a more hands-off model, in which gardening beds are provided to local community members who then take personal responsibility for the space. Other congregations see gardening as a church program that involves budgeting, planned events, and organizing volunteers. This more active approach should include conversation with local partners about what foods would

14 Tobi White, email correspondence with authors, August 28, 2024.

be most appreciated and long-term reflection on how to sustain the ministry and avoid burnout among volunteers. If a community garden seems like a stretch, then congregations might get connected with a group like Interfaith Power & Light, which is a national organization that offers ideas and resources for congregations to engage climate change and practice environmental stewardship at the grassroots level.[15]

REAL-LIFE STORIES OF FOOD AND VOCATION

Food theology offers a valuable framework to understand and affirm the many ways that people live out their faith in God and love of neighbors by serving and nourishing their communities. While this chapter has already given some examples of individuals and congregations who share God's love through gardening, the next section will provide additional stories of people who are called to the abundant, faith-filled, and often challenging work of proclaiming God's care for creation through a small sampling of food-related vocations. Far from being an exhaustive list of the many vocations within the realm of food theology, these stories are offered with a spirit of encouragement and mutual support. These stories may inspire you to consider a new way to engage your community, or to seek out others who are already doing the work of food theology and explore how you can join them, or to amplify and advocate for the hungers you see around you. These examples also invite you to think about how you would tell your own stories of food theology as testimony to God's love at work in your life. As always, starting where we are, with what we already have, is a foundational perspective of food theology, leading us to better understand the triune God, ourselves, and all of God's beloved creation.

---

15 Interfaith Power & Light, accessed June 2024, https://interfaithpowerandlight.org/.

Soup Kitchens

Jeri Kraver has volunteered at local food ministries for the better part of the last two decades. She knows the challenges faced by hungry people and people who plan and prepare food, as well as the institutions who support, sponsor, and host the ministries. She currently serves at the Loveland Community Kitchen in Loveland, Colorado, where she shows up twice each week, serving in weather that ranges from three feet of snow to scorching 95-degree heat. Jeri works the Sunday afternoon and Tuesday evening shifts alongside her dedicated core team, which includes Gary and Wendy, each of whom function in different roles during their shifts together and who make Sunday afternoons a favorite for the guests who come to eat. The guests often pronounce, "Sunday crew's the best crew!" which is likely due to the way Jeri and her team approach their work. "I'm there to treat them with dignity," Jeri says. "Any little things we can do? Let's do those things." From this perspective comes an innate valuing of each person who comes to eat. Jeri and her team know folks' dietary needs, know their names, know what they like to drink, offer choice whenever possible, make sure things like salad dressing are served on the side, feed the dogs that come to sit under the table with their owners, take effort to roll silverware up nicely in napkins, listen to what people need, and offer assistance when possible.

For Jeri, it is not just about tending to physical hunger but also about truly seeing each person. She notes that balancing human needs with the financial challenges of the institutions that support the daily meals sometimes leads to conflicting priorities. In such cases, she works to lead with creativity, making the most of what is available and offering more empowering suggestions when institutional rules might threaten the dignity of their volunteers or the people they serve.

She has observed a trajectory of poverty through her decades spent working in the kitchens and dining rooms of food ministries. Some guests who come to eat are homeless, while others have run out of money at the end of the month. Some guests are actively working in society to get themselves what they need, while others are entrenched in social and economic constraints that they are unable to escape. Regardless of the circumstances that lead people to be guests at the daily meal, Jeri notes that all people are in need of relationship and of the act of eating in the company of others. She calls it a "food connection," as camaraderie takes place around a table.

While some people who volunteer only come once, Jeri is aware of the difference a committed, regular volunteer can make. There is a much greater capacity for growth and effectiveness when volunteers want to learn, truly care for the guests, and can routinely show up. This creates better communication among each night's service team, better execution of daily tasks, and a stronger buy-in to the big picture of the work, all of which makes a big difference for everyone involved. When volunteers become regular, they also have the chance to learn the stories of the guests. Jeri notes, "When you know their stories, you can stop judging them. You hear their stories, hear their sadness, and you feed them." Serving the guests from this perspective is an embodiment of her Jewish faith and an expression of love for humanity. Jeri states, "We don't have to do big things, but we can do small things that make a big difference."[16]

Agricultural Journalism

Alan Guebert grew up on a family farm near where the Kaskaskia River flows into the Mississippi River in West Central Illinois. He has worked as an agricultural journalist since 1980 and written an award-winning, nationally syndicated column about agricultural policy and rural life since 1993. With his daughter Mary Grace Foxwell, Guebert published a collection of his writings in his book *The Land of Milk and Uncle Honey: Memories from the Farm of My Youth*. While the book largely revolves around seasonal life on the

16 Jeri Kraver, in discussion with the authors, August 27, 2024.

farm and tells stories of colorful characters like Uncle Honey and cherished farmhands like Howard and Jackie, Alan also describes the culture of work and faith that his parents nurtured. Along with the rhythms of dairy farming, his family faithfully made the twenty-minute drive to church on Sundays and held daily devotions in the home at mealtimes.

By paying attention not only to influential agricultural voices but to people like the "hired men" on the farm whose wisdom and friendship also enriched his perspectives, Guebert's columns continue to honestly discuss how the consolidation now common in the agricultural industry has impacted rural communities, often to the detriment of small-town economies and agricultural workers. Through it all, Alan reflects on what it means to be called to a food-oriented vocation, writing, "Work was (is) a big part of life and life was (is) a gift from God. As such, work was (is) part of God's good plan for you and your happiness."[17] This elegant summary of the meaning of vocation—serving God and neighbors in daily life—quietly yet consistently reached him through the witness of his parents. Although religious experiences and teachings are secondary themes in Guebert's book and his weekly columns, deeply rooted themes of thankfulness to God for life, appreciation for the land, and care for healthy communities add a warm touch of personal dedication to his otherwise more technical writing in the field of agricultural journalism.

Care for Neighbors

Many people engage in the regular work of providing care for others through food in their local community and friend groups. These folks are quick to drop by cookies to a new person on the block, start

---

17 Guebert with Foxwell, *Milk and Uncle Honey*, 6. Responses are also informed by email correspondence between Mr. Guebert and the authors of this book (January 8, 2021 and January 21, 2021).

a Meal Train to invite others to support with meals while a friend recovers from surgery, or bring a frozen casserole to new parents. While friendship between neighbors is perhaps less common now than it was in years past, the language that expresses care through food has not diminished. Expressing this type of care goes a long way toward meeting people's basic needs of hunger and thirst—physiological needs that are a necessity for all living beings. Meeting hunger needs also has the power to support people as they live into other parts of themselves, creating space for people to experience safety and belonging.

This section on care for neighbors as a food vocation could carry any number of names. There are many ways to express care through food, and it is likely that you have both shared with others in this way and had others share with you. The opportunities are endless: bake an extra loaf of banana bread, send home kolacky for baking at dinner time, feed neighborhood kids snacks after school, bring coffee to a colleague, provide loaves of bread and peanut butter and jelly in a classroom for emergency lunches, prepare twice the quantity of a meal so that an extra meal can be dropped off for a friend in the midst of a busy week, send a gift card for food delivery to a friend out of state, deliver breakfast items to teachers at the local elementary school, keep snacks on hand in your desk for the student who comes to school hungry, volunteer to fill backpacks with school supplies and food, and drop by with sandwiches for a friend "just because." These are but a few examples of heartfelt actions that not only express care but embody the principles of food theology. Moments of care such as these also create deep relationships, promoting much-needed belonging and well-being.

When we understand food vocations through small daily activities, the role we each can play in enacting food theology in our own contexts of home, church, school, work, and neighborhood becomes even more clear. No action is too small, and all care carries with it the love of God who works in, among, and through us.

Beekeeping

Charlie "Charbee" Koenen spreads the gospel of abundance as taught by the bees through advocacy, education, products, and practice.[18] Located on the roof of Redeemer Lutheran Church in downtown Milwaukee, Wisconsin, Charlie tends to beehives that he uses for production, education, and environmental care. Students, aspiring beekeepers, local neighbors, and curious visitors can often be found tending the bees with him on the roof of Redeemer. A gregarious, friendly presence in the community, Charlie brings a calm steadiness to the beekeeping world he manages. Visitors frequently handle the frames of the hives without suits or gloves, and stings are rare. Koenen values his relationship and oneness with the bees, understanding their important role in our ecosystem and creating products like candles, lip balm, and honey in partnership with the bees' natural production. He understands the bees as communal creators, driven by abundance, and in harmony with all creation as he invites others to share in stewarding the work of the bees.

An important partnership in Charlie's "beevangelism" developed with the people of Redeemer.[19] Charlie has reflected on how during that partnership, he and Pastor Lisa Bates-Froiland would talk about the hive. As a result of those talks, Pastor Lisa often "would find a correlation to scripture and weave it into her sermons. We became like the bees, coming to the hive for service and spiritual nourishment then going out, spreading the gospel of abundance and diversity. . . . Redeemer became the Hive of Activity."[20] The collaboration between Charlie and Redeemer has in many ways been sweet and nourishing as honey, creating space for congregants and visitors to be in communal partnership with the busy working bees.

---

18 Beevangelists, accessed August 2024, https://beevangelists.org/.

19 Redeemer Lutheran Church, accessed August 2024, https://www.redeemermilwaukee.org/.

20 Charlie Koenen, email correspondence with the authors, August 23, 2024.

Cooking for Large Groups

Chris Seaman has been cooking at Rainbow Trail Lutheran Camp in Hillside, Colorado, for over two decades. She came to camp with years of food preparation experience, which she funneled into her work on the mountain. Her delicious cooking is a basis for the camp's food philosophy, which is taught during staff training, and emphasized in every single meal throughout a camper's week: if a camper enjoys the food, their camp experience is much more likely to go well. At Rainbow Trail, the leadership knows that a person's experience at camp is either helped or hindered by the quality of the food. They also know that well-fed campers are going to feel better, engage more, and truly immerse themselves in the camp experience. Therefore, feeding people well is prioritized and the experience of abundance is felt throughout each day. Chris tends to all food allergies and dietary needs, bakes fresh bread for every dinner, and ensures there is enough food for hungry campers and staff to have second helpings, all while making efforts to minimize waste.

Far from an isolated space controlled by a head chef, Chris's kitchen is a hospitable space filled with photographs of the camp staff from past summers, with everything well labeled and in its place. There are enough aprons for anyone who pops by the kitchen to help, and long counters that create an inviting workspace. The kitchen is often full of staff and campers immersed in work and in conversation. Just as in many homes, the kitchen is the place where people want to be, knowing that they are welcome, that there is enough for them, and that there is a task waiting for them if they but ask to help.

VOCATION AS BEING EMBEDDED IN THE WORLD

Such contributions to the common good show how there are many opportunities to serve God and neighbor in a variety of professional and personal settings. As VanLaningham wrote about the connections that happen through our varied vocations: "When we talk about what we do, what we love, what nourishes us, and what we care about, we are talking about our embeddedness within the world. We live within and are dependent upon larger structures that connect us to each other and the environment."[21] In vocations of food theology, our connectedness is clear. We are intricately connected to the seeds, the crops, the rain, the sun, the bees, the laborers, the processors, the packagers, the suppliers, the grocery store stockers, and the cashiers. If one piece of our interwoven food web fails, we all fall. We are deeply connected to one another, to the earth, and to all of creation.

Our awareness of how we are embedded in the world can lead us into positive action, such as advocacy, growing food, paying attention to what and how we eat, noticing who is hungry, and not taking more than our fair share. From a soup kitchen or pollinator education to growing a tomato on your deck or herbs in your windowsill, there are many ways to be involved in stewarding God's gift of food and care for the earth. While very few of us will be syndicated agribusiness columnists, cook three meals a day at summer camp, or establish beehives on the roofs of urban churches, we can all practice vocations of food theology in our own ways, living into the words of Jesus's Sermon on the Mount: "let your light shine before others, so that they may see your good works and give glory to your Father in heaven."[22]

MEALS FROM THE GARDEN

Simple, delicious meals are made easy when you have vegetables from a local garden, farmer's market, food pantry, or grocery store. Salads are a natural fit when you consider how to use the vegetables you might find in your backyard or on the produce aisle. Although

21 VanLaningham, *Called Beyond Our Selves*, 304.

22 Matt 5:16.

salad is sometimes thought to be a boring or bland afterthought, the examples that follow suggest tasty ways to make refreshing use of whatever abundant harvests you have on hand.

Generally, a great salad will have one ingredient from each of the following categories: salty, sweet, creamy, acidic, crunchy, and fresh.[23] This results in a salad that hits all the flavor profiles and textures, making you want to dig your fork back in for more! As you think about combining ingredients to make your own salads, begin with what you have that could fit into each of the following categories, and remember that "categories" are flexible and can be loosely held depending on your own flavor and texture desires.

- Salty: nuts, olives, capers, sunflower seeds, pepitas
- Sweet: fruit, dressing, candied nuts, raisins
- Creamy: cheese, dressing, avocado, beans, hard boiled eggs, mayonnaise-based tuna or egg salad, fried egg with runny yolk
- Acidic: citrus juice, mustard, vinegar, pickled vegetables, pepperoncini
- Crunchy: croutons, sunflower seeds, nuts, peppers, breadcrumbs, roasted chickpeas
- Fresh: lettuce, tomato, zucchini, asparagus, cucumber

With the above categories in mind, here are a few examples of how these simple ingredients could come together to make something fantastic. Each base example is gluten free and vegan, and depending on your own dietary needs, a few tasty optional add-ins are listed as well. Following these examples are recipe strategies for a few basic dressings, as well as croutons, roasted chickpeas, and candied nuts, all of which make an excellent topping or dressing for salad!

23 To learn more about how to combine flavors and textures, see, *Salt, Fat, Acid, Heat: Mastering the Elements of Good Cooking* by Samin Nosrat.

Tangy Salad with Nuts and Vinaigrette

Start with green or red leaf lettuce or mixed greens. You can then make a salad that is both sweet and tangy by using the following ideas for making candied nuts and a maple syrup vinaigrette. Optional additions can include grilled or skillet-browned chicken, sliced red onion, diced green apple, and feta or blue cheese crumbles.

Almonds, walnuts, pecans, and cashews are all delicious when candied. The basic process goes like this: roughly chop the nuts (one or two cups, depending on desired quantity), then add to a skillet warmed over low heat. Allow the nuts to lightly toast as you frequently and gently shake the skillet back and forth (or stir with a spatula) to keep any side of the nuts from burning. Do this for about three minutes. For each cup of nuts in the skillet, add one tablespoon of water along with two tablespoons of sugar and a quarter of a teaspoon of kosher salt. Stir well with a spatula, allowing the sugar to dissolve and thoroughly coat the nuts. Prepare a layer of parchment paper or a silicone mat on the counter. Once the nuts have reached the desired toastiness—about three minutes—spread the mixture on the prepared surface. Allow the nuts to cool to the touch, then break up any clusters with clean hands.

These candied nuts can be added directly to salads or eaten on their own. Variations on this simple strategy include switching white sugar to brown sugar and adding a teaspoon of cinnamon, along with a sprinkle of nutmeg, for spiced nuts. Spiced nuts would make a great salad topper paired with baby lettuce, roasted butternut squash, red onion, goat or blue cheese, and the vinaigrette recipe below.

A mason jar with a lid is a great vessel for making salad dressings in, and it makes storage a breeze as well. Begin with a small dollop of mustard—Dijon or whole grain mustard are both tasty options—then add about a quarter of a cup of pure maple syrup. One teaspoon of kosher salt, eight grinds of black pepper, and around one-third of a cup of white wine vinegar[24] can join the party in the jar. Mix well,

24 Apple cider vinegar is also a delicious option here.

using a fork, then slowly drizzle in around two-thirds of a cup of olive oil, briskly mixing with the fork as you drizzle in the oil. This quantity of dressing will be enough for several salads. Simply add one tablespoon of dressing to each serving of salad and toss well.

With this dressing, the candied nuts, and any of the optional add-ins noted above, you will have a salad that is sweet, tangy, crunchy, and satisfying.

Mediterranean Salad

Salads that use ingredients typical of Mediterranean cuisines like olives, chickpeas (also called garbanzo beans), and cucumbers are enjoyable either as a zesty side dish or as a filling main dish when served with protein and a grain. For these salads, use romaine, green or red leaf lettuce, kalamata olives, cucumbers, pepperoncini, tomatoes, roasted chickpeas, and an herby vinaigrette dressing.

If desired, feta cheese crumbles can add extra texture and flavor. Grains can either complement the salad on the side, with items like pita bread, pita chips, or naan, or can be added into the salad as cooked quinoa or couscous. The following dressing and roasted chickpeas will top it off brilliantly.

Again, begin with a mason jar. This time, add a dollop of Dijon mustard and a teaspoon each of the following: kosher salt, dried basil, powdered garlic, powdered onion, dried parsley, and white sugar. Add one tablespoon of dried oregano and about one-third of a cup of red wine vinegar. Mix well, using a fork, then slowly drizzle in around two-thirds of a cup of olive oil, briskly mixing with the fork as you drizzle in the oil. Again, approximately one tablespoon of dressing will dress each serving of salad.

To roast chickpeas, preheat the oven to 400 degrees. Drain and rinse two cans of garbanzo beans and spread them out on a rimmed baking sheet. You can line the baking sheet with parchment or aluminum foil for easier cleanup. Coat the beans with a healthy drizzle of olive oil and sprinkle with around one teaspoon each of the following: kosher salt, garlic powder, paprika, and oregano. Toss with a spatula or clean hands. Place the baking sheet in the center of the oven and roast for around thirty minutes, removing the baking sheet at the halfway point to gently shake the chickpeas so that they wiggle around for more even crisping. Remove the chickpeas from the oven when they reach desired level of crispiness. These are delightful on their own as a high-protein snack, and they also make a perfect addition to a Mediterranean salad. Leftover chickpeas can be stored in an airtight container in the refrigerator. You can change the flavor profile of the chickpeas by mixing up the spice combo: just use one teaspoon of each spice you'd like to use.

Tortilla Chip Salad

This Mexican-inspired salad is tasty and filling. It also allows you to use a wide variety of random vegetables, as well as the salty crumbles at the bottom of the tortilla chip bag. Start with green leaf or romaine lettuce, then mix in a combination of ingredients like corn, black beans, tomato, and black olives. You can also add chopped vegetables such as zucchini, bell peppers, and avocado. Serve with crushed corn tortilla chips on top or with strips of lightly fried tortillas. Lightly frying the tortillas has the advantage of freshening up old or stale tortillas that might otherwise not get used. If cheese is desired, then consider adding crumbles or grates of cheddar or Oaxaca cheese. Dollops of salsa, green chili, sour cream, and/or guacamole make a great dressing for this salad.

Forgotten Salad

Salad can be a great way to use a variety of vegetables that might otherwise not be a first choice for mealtimes. Take whatever is lingering in the crisper drawer, chop it up, and give it a simple dressing of kosher salt, ground black pepper, vinegar (i.e., red wine, white wine, or apple cider vinegar), and olive oil. Flakes and peels of parmesan, Manchego, or Romano cheese can add flavor and depth to this celebration of forgotten veggies. Croutons can be made from stale bread in a manner very similar to the roasted chickpeas recipe above.

Preheat the oven to 400 degrees. Roughly tear or cube whatever bread you have on hand, about five cups worth, and spread it out on a rimmed baking sheet. You can line the baking sheet with parchment or aluminum foil for easier cleanup, if you like. Coat the bread with five tablespoons of olive oil (one for each cup of bread) and sprinkle with around one teaspoon each of kosher salt, garlic powder, and paprika, plus two teaspoons of oregano. Toss with a flat spatula or your clean hands. Place in the center of the oven and toast for twelve to fourteen minutes, removing from the oven at the halfway point and flipping the breach chunks with the spatula. This will allow for more even toasting. Once golden and toasted, remove croutons from oven and allow to cool slightly before adding to salad. Leftover croutons can be placed in a sealed container for later use.

CONCLUSION: CLAIMING OUR FOOD VOCATIONS

In each of these salad recipes, a wide variety of foods come together to create a meal that bursts with flavor and brings out the best in each ingredient. In a similar way, each one of us has unique contributions to make to the world around us. We honor God our Good Gardener and serve our neighbors by sharing our talents and gifts with those around us. Whether you like to grow food or prepare it, share a recipe or a conversation, work closely with food every day or just enjoy eating it, God has given us many ways to live together in love.

Gathered around the table, we can connect back to our human roots and remember that, like Adam and Eve before us, we are born from the soil, created to live within and alongside all of creation. We can acknowledge that, even as we know that we live in imperfect systems in an imperfect world, a perspective of food theology makes space for nourishing abundance and allows us to consider our own relationship and role with food, creation, and one another in a grace-filled, life-giving way.

CONVERSATION AROUND THE TABLE

1. How might you already be participating in a food-related vocation?
2. Who do you know from your community who serves in a food-related vocation? What seems life-giving or challenging about that work? How do you, or could you, partner with them in their work?
3. What soup kitchens or food-related ministries are nearby? Can you visit to join in service or in a meal?
4. What is your favorite way to use fresh produce from the garden or grocery store?
5. What farms or community gardens are closest to you? Do you get produce from them?

CHAPTER 6

Dinner Church

PRAYER

Revealing God,
Thank you for the bountiful table which you prepare.
May our fellowship reflect your care:
Beloved people gathered, united, and nourished
Friends at your table of love and service.
Amen.

INTRODUCTION: MEALS THAT REVEAL JESUS

In the early church, before the cross became a prominent symbol for Christian salvation and restoration, food expressed the power and significance of Jesus's salvation in tasteable, touchable ways. Jesus himself talked about being "the bread of life" and the one who gives "living water." Although loaves of bread have not made it onto the tops of steeples or popular forms of religious jewelry like crosses have, bread and cups are powerful symbols of the real transformation that Jesus brings through the gift of food and drink, as seen in the current chalice logo of the Christian Church (Disciples of Christ).[1]

1 "The Chalice," Christian Church (Disciples of Christ) in the United States and Canada, accessed August 2024, https://disciples.org/our-identity/the-chalice/.

As discussed in previous chapters, food can indeed be a blessing that unites, orients, shifts, and creates in Jesus's name. Jesus revealed God's loving care in breakfast on the beach, in bread and wine around the table, and in small offerings of loaves and fishes transformed into miraculous abundance. Similarly, the risen Christ shared a meal of hospitality after talking with amazed disciples on the road to Emmaus. It was a meal that revealed Jesus.

As Luke 24 relates, on that first Easter two disciples were walking from Jerusalem to Emmaus when they encountered Jesus, risen from the dead. Although the story does not say why these followers of Jesus did not immediately recognize him, the grief of recent days could have played a part in clouding their eyes and hearts. While they continued walking, Jesus led these disciples through an interpretation of Scripture that connected the crucifixion they had just witnessed with biblical promises about the messiah. Reaching their destination for the night, the two disciples invited Jesus to stay with them. "When he was at the table with them, he took bread, blessed and broke it, and gave it to them. Then their eyes were opened, and they recognized him; and he vanished from their sight."[2] Filled with the holy joy of that meal, the two disciples hurried back to Jerusalem to tell the other disciples, describing "what had happened on the road, and how he had been made known to them in the breaking of the bread."[3]

This story of the road to Emmaus provides a helpful introduction to contemporary practices of Dinner Church gatherings that combine a service of Holy Communion with a full community meal.[4] While the Dinner Church label may be new to some readers, the practice revolves around familiar elements of word and sacrament. It is marked from beginning to end by serving, singing, praying, and sharing; gifts and activities that reveal Jesus Christ alive and active in our midst.

---

2 Luke 24:30–31.

3 Luke 24:35.

4 Dinner Church is capitalized in this chapter in recognition of its status as an intentional practice in contemporary North American Christianity.

MEALS THAT REVEAL GOD'S LOVE

Contemporary ministries called Dinner Church have origins with the Community Dinners led by Verlon Fosner in Seattle in 2007[5] and with St. Lydia's Dinner Church in Brooklyn, New York, organized by Emily Scott and Rachel Kroh in 2008.[6] In addition to addressing personal hungers, these communities have been intentional about feeding the hunger for relationships, the longing for interpersonal connection that is deeply embedded in our human experience. As Pastor Scott described the budding Dinner Church community in her book *For All Who Hunger*, "We all cook and set up for dinner together. . . . We sing and light candles, and I bless the bread, and we share it. We eat, talk about scripture, and share our stories. And then we hold hands and pray, clean up together, get a blessing, and go home."[7] She and Rachel Kroh asked each other as they imagined a community like this: "Is it possible to create a church that's made of real life?"[8]

Holy Communion connects us to God and to each other as the body of Christ becomes an accessible, edible promise. At the same time, we have also seen how an ordinary plate of hot food, the inviting smell of warm fresh bread, and conversations over refreshments all reveal the power of God at work in our bodies, lives, and communities. Through participation in holy meals of all kinds, congregations and communities get to experience and extend the generous hospitality that Jesus did. We learn to see Christ's presence in our midst in surprising ways and at unexpected tables, just as the disciples recognized Jesus in the breaking of the bread. As Pastor Scott observed, God has blessed food with the power to connect the Holy Spirit's ongoing activity with the parts of real life that might not easily come to the surface in worship settings.

---

5 "About Us," Community Dinners, accessed June 2024, https://www.communitydinners.com/about-us/.

6 For more about St. Lydia's Dinner Church, see Scott, *For All Who Hunger*. See also, St. Lydia's, accessed June 2024, https://stlydias.org/.

7 Scott, 8.

8 Scott, 39.

These divine blessings are embodied in Dinner Church, which is an expanded celebration of Holy Communion. After some time for gathering, the service begins with the bread of Christ's own self, continues with a full meal and the sharing of Christ's cup, and then closes with refreshed hearts going out to serve others, beginning with cleaning up in the kitchen, tidying the space, and saying friendly goodbyes. As an extended experience of the Eucharist shared in a community meal, Dinner Church brings sustained focus to the many ways God's grace is given in worship and fellowship.

In recent years, ministries like those started at Community Dinners and St. Lydia's have named and popularized Dinner Church in significant ways. At the same time, it is important to honor the many ways that gathering around the table for the purpose of worship has been practiced throughout history. Jewish celebrations of Passover and other community meals of the Jewish tradition existed long before the start of Christianity and continue in inspiring and enriching ways to this day. Other social and religious groups in the Mediterranean region of Jesus's time also gathered around meals to share teachings and fellowship. Indeed, it is very likely that early Christian Communion practices followed the patterns of "meal fellowship" in the Greco-Roman world, perhaps with a strong focus on the radical sharing of resources or the creation of new egalitarian communities as key traits of the early Jesus movement.[9] Dinner Church practices vary at each congregation where it has been adopted, yet the experience consistently provides an embodied, nourishing entrance into the way of Jesus Christ, who revealed himself at meals along roadsides, on mountainsides, amid crowded cities, and in humble homes.

REAL-LIFE RESOURCES: ENACTING DINNER CHURCH

The following sections describe the multifaceted goals of Dinner Church and offer practical guidance for planning and hosting

---

9 Lathrop, *Four Gospels on Sunday*, 40–43. See also, Taussig, *Beginning Was the Meal*, 21–54.

such a meal. Aspects of the previous chapters come together here, including paying attention to how we prepare, gather, worship, eat, and serve. By viewing the activities around preparing a meal, the act of sharing food, and the activities involved in meal cleanup as worshipful moments, participants experience the holiness that fills everyday habits, actions, and bodily needs, revealing profound closeness with God and each other. This shift in perception helps us recognize God's continual love for the world, even in daily activities such as shopping, setting tables, cooking, sharing food, and spending time together.

There is no one-size-fits-all model when it comes to creating a Dinner Church ministry, as each context will have specific needs, hungers, and gifts that will help the experience come to life in authentic and faithful ways. What follows here, then, is not a single tried-and-true recipe, but rather a set of strategies to guide the way. Just as each cook will adapt a recipe based on what they know, want, and have on hand, so too should each Dinner Church leader approach their setting. As always, begin where you are and consider what you have. This approach will serve you and your community well by focusing on the blessings and opportunities that are already at hand.

Planning Worship

Dinner Church is literally a church service that happens over dinner. The following pattern for the worship service offers an adaptable structure and flow. You can expect the experience to come to life as you compose a liturgy that speaks to the uniqueness of your context, mixing new and familiar words to draw meaning from local traditions and to nourish faithful lives. Other details for Dinner Church preparation, such as leadership, space setup, food, and more will be discussed later in this chapter. For now, we begin with the flow of the service so that you can begin to imagine what a Dinner Church service might look and sound like in your own setting.

The service can begin with opening words of Scripture and a simple response. To minimize the use of paper, no one but the worship leaders needs to have printed materials. In this instance, simplicity is a virtue. For instance, as people find their seats, the leader can teach them their line, something like, "Nourish us, Lord," which could be the response to a verse like Ecclesiastes 9:7: "Go, eat your bread with enjoyment, and drink your wine with a merry heart; for God has long ago approved what you do." Another way to combine materials and worship planning is to print the liturgy, or portions of it, as place mats.

Words of welcome and an explanation of the flow of the meal can be followed by the distribution of candles (or battery-powered lights for young children), which are lit as people prepare for an opening prayer and a simple song that can be easily taught and sung. After the song, the lit candles can be carefully placed in vessels filled with sand, so that dinner takes place by candlelight.

After worshippers have taken their seats, the bread is blessed. This is a different pattern than the usual Sunday morning liturgy, as the eucharistic prayers that bless the bread happen right away in Dinner Church. Blessed and broken, the bread is shared around tables, with each person communing their neighbor with the words, "The body of Christ, given for you," or with similar words that fit your context. Having been fed with Christ, the rest of the community dinner is now shared, with the focus on grateful eating and neighborly conversation.

Without rushing people, about ten minutes can be given so that most people can eat most of their food. Another simple song or musical offering might provide a transition from eating and conversation to a reading from Scripture and a gospel-centered sermon. To keep the convivial atmosphere alive while someone preaches, the sermon can be accompanied by opportunities to doodle; take notes; have dialogue with the preacher; or sample light desserts, coffee, or other after-dinner enjoyments. The Prayers of the People come next, shared in whatever way the community best prays together, perhaps with some balance of having a prayer leader and inviting people to add their petitions.

The prayers conclude with the eucharistic blessing of the cup and the Lord's Prayer. People then drink the wine or grape juice that has been set before them for this purpose. Pouring from pitchers into individual reusable cups offers a visible sign of unity, a way to practice good hygiene, and a practical step to reduce plastic waste. Together, people hear the words, "The blood of Christ, shed for you" (or, again, other liturgical language for your context) and share in this cup of grace.

Worship then shifts into service as the fellowship of cleaning up begins and conversation continues. Blowing out the candles reminds us that the light of Christ and the promises of baptism continue to live inside us and shine through us. As the work concludes, people come back together to close the meal with another song and prayer, and those who have eaten together are sent out renewed and strengthened in faith, friendship, service, and love.

Invitations to Lead

Alongside an understanding of the theological and liturgical basis of Dinner Church and with your own basic strategy in mind, it is important to plan how to invite people into the experience. One good place to start as you consider building a new food-related ministry like Dinner Church is to ask: What are the people in your community or congregation hungry for? While many community members may certainly hunger for good food, it is possible that even more may hunger to know their neighbors and to be known themselves. The hunger for connection and belonging is an age-old desire that Dinner Church is uniquely poised to meet.

These longings for fellowship can be true for churches that are both newer and more established. Older congregations that have gone through recent hardships, transitions, or turnover might enjoy and benefit from new ways to reconnect and rebuild relationships.

Additional questions to ask when learning what people are hungering for include:

- How easy is it for new people to feel included or get involved in your congregation? Could it happen relatively quickly, or does it seem to take years?
- What opportunities do people without nearby family or other social networks have to eat with other people and make new friends?
- Is the congregation aware of the rhythms of the neighborhood or of people who might not be able to attend worship on Sunday mornings?
- Who is invited into leadership roles? Who is missing from leadership?

With such questions in mind, you can identify the people who will come alongside you to help make things happen. Maybe this means sharing your ideas with leaders who plan worship and with volunteers who frequently use the church kitchen. What interests or concerns do they have? Who in the community might share your passion and help something get started? What kind of donations or funding might be helpful? Good partners who support a mealtime ministry (or who agree not to get in the way of it, at least!) are tremendous blessings. It is also nice to let them know you appreciate their support as plans get underway.

Because Dinner Church is both food and worship, it invites team building. A few people might plan the worship aspect of the gathering. Depending on the congregation, this could include pastors or deacons, music ministers, and members of worship or outreach committees. Others can plan the menu and organize volunteers for cooking. Still other people might enjoy preparing the space to be as warm and welcoming as possible. As is often true with event planning, a mixture of familiar and new elements can help stir up an experience that is at once inviting and inspiring.

Guest-Centered Planning

Many people today are suffering from loneliness, isolation, and lack of connection, a situation that has been identified as a public health crisis.[10] At the same time, many individuals and families find themselves with packed schedules and little time for social activities or personal refreshment. For both reasons, consider what nights people are more likely to be available for church events. How might an alternative worship service like Dinner Church build upon existing opportunities to come together? Integrating Dinner Church into other church programming or activity times can help facilitate a good overall experience for individuals and families, demonstrating respect for people's time and energy. This can make the meal even more important as it brings together people with busy lives, those in need of a good meal, families who desire quality time together, and volunteers who regularly give of themselves for the life of the community, offering people with a variety of life situations the ability to show up fully and to go home refreshed.

At least at the beginning, it can be helpful to know how many people to expect. Without being rigid about RSVPs or reservations, creating an online or paper sign-up form can provide a good estimation of how many place settings and meal servings to prepare. These forms can be advertised in existing community resources, like social media pages, church emails and bulletin boards, and announcements at worship services, with the understanding that numbers will be reasonably flexible.

Along with planning what to serve, it is worth thinking beforehand how to serve the meal and prepare the space so that it feels warm and inviting. Many churches already have decorative items like vases, tablecloths, wreaths, strings of lights, and battery-lit candles that can create an inviting space. While some of these

10 "Our Epidemic of Loneliness and Isolation: The U.S. Surgeon General's Advisory on the Healing Effects of Social Connection and Community," 2023, accessed March 21, 2025, https://www.hhs.gov/sites/default/files/surgeon-general-social-connection-advisory.pdf

decorative elements might be as shrouded in mystery as the dusty cabinets and closets in which they are found, some could have unique stories attached to them: a wreath made from a church member's tree, a candelabra or Communion ware dedicated to a beloved parishioner who passed away, a table setting made years earlier by the youth group. These little touches can be rightly celebrated and their stories told, as honoring the history of the objects lets people know that they are in a community that celebrates and acknowledges one another, both valuing their past and excited about where they are going next.

To address important hungers like belonging and fellowship, consider the welcome that is extended by the space and the people. As discussed in previous chapters, issues of accessibility and clear signage are helpful; name tags help remove the embarrassment of not knowing everyone's names. Take time to consider the many pieces of your Dinner Church strategy, so that you have what you need to develop a meaningful worship experience.

Accommodating Dietary Needs

Dinner Church can function differently from a potluck. In a potluck, the amount of food available is organically matched to the amount of people present. While Dinner Church certainly might include a potluck meal, an alternative is to prepare a meal that can be served by the table (sometimes called "family-style"), which enhances experiences of connection and belonging. If using this format, a participant sign-up sheet not only gives the planners a good idea of how much food to prepare but also provides a simple way to learn about food allergies or other dietary needs in advance. Acknowledging and working with different dietary needs is an important part of Dinner Church hospitality. Because we believe that the grace of God is abundant for all, we can communicate that care through the food we serve, ensuring that our meal is accessible and nourishing for all who come. If learning about potential food restrictions from a list is not an easy option, some congregational leaders might already have a good grasp of the allergies or other dietary restrictions that exist in the community. Even if you cannot predict all the needs your community might face, a general statement communicating that all are welcome and that known food restrictions will be honored will help foster a welcoming atmosphere.

Some common dietary restrictions are noted in appendix 1, along with simple recipe swaps that can promote safety for people with food allergies. Of course, communicating directly with your people is the best approach, because they will have experience cooking for themselves, can offer suggestions, and might appreciate being asked to join in the planning or cooking of these inclusive meals. Preparing an "allergen-free" serving table can be a simple way to practice food safety and hospitality. For instance, if your community serves the pot pie meal described at the end of this chapter, and you have community members who need a gluten-free or vegan meal, then dishes of the pot pie with a wheat-based crust can be passed at the table, while the gluten-free and vegan version can be provided at another easily accessible table off to the side. Anyone who needs the allergen-free dish can easily get to it while others from their table are collecting their serving dishes for the tables. This allows folks to have access to the food they need, while staying connected to the rest of the group.

In a similar sign of care for the community, those who prepare the meal should read food labels carefully and fully disclose what is on the menu. This will be an additional aid to those with dietary restrictions. One fun way to share this information is to create a menu to post on the wall for people to read in advance and during the meal. The menu can describe every item being served, listing all the ingredients in each item, so that people can make safe decisions for themselves. In addition to being a valuable health feature, the menu could also become a creative way to advertise the great food you will be sharing!

Nutritious and Delicious

What about the food itself? A Dinner Church meal can take a variety of shapes: it can be a potluck, pizza delivery, a home-cooked meal prepared by one person ahead of time, or a group production with people working in the kitchen together. Variety of practice is built into the Dinner Church model, but amid that diversity, there are some best practices to consider and share.

First, something transformational happens when people gather to cook a meal. While working with a team can bring some logistical challenges, it can also foster deep relationships, a stronger sense of intentionality, increased personal investment in the event, skill building, and tons of fun. Cooking together can shift meal preparation from a chore to an extension of worship.

With that in mind, it is good to create opportunities for leadership and participation through meal preparation. For instance, a meal prep team of four to six individuals could be invited to rotate among themselves when it comes to providing a main dish and various sides. A team that works together in the kitchen might alternate who serves as the lead cook and delegates tasks or there may be one key leader who plans the meals and leads the cook teams each week. However you choose to structure the leadership of the cook teams, magic will happen when the teams come together in the kitchen. As the group members chop and stir, they will also talk, sharing the struggles, joys, questions, and challenges that fill their lives. Matters of faith and God in their lives may naturally come up, so that many layers of interpersonal and communal relationships can be built and fortified.

When people prepare a meal together, they forge deeper connections to each other. They can also learn important cooking skills. Regardless of previous experience (or inexperience), team members can learn or teach skills such as how to chop an onion, mince garlic, and prepare chicken stock. They can learn how to wash dishes, follow a recipe, and rinse lettuce. Participating in cooking teams not only builds interpersonal relationships but also self-reliance as members become more confident and capable when it comes to enjoying the gifts of food and community that God blesses them with. These skills, learned around the table of the Lord in the context of worship and community, will last long after a meal is over, benefiting them all their lives.

Whatever meal and style of serving your group chooses, it is best to make recipes that are straightforward, nourishing, full of flavor, and easily scalable for large groups. Soup is always a great option, as are casseroles. It also helps to find recipes that can be easily adapted to accommodate food allergy needs. The meal will fill the air with its scents and define the work that hands will do, enriching both the dining experience and the worship experience.

Like preparing a good meal, there are many ways to plan worship in nourishing ways, inviting people into a shared experience of God and holy community with both intentionality and openness. The fourth-century bishop Augustine of Hippo once wrote that good theology is like nutritious food: everyone needs it, but sometimes it helps if it is presented in tasty ways. In his words, "Learning has a lot in common with eating: to cater for the dislikes of the majority even the nutrients essential for life must be made appetizing."[11]

In that spirit, the meal presented at the end of this chapter includes a satisfying main dish and a scrumptious side of vegetables. Don't skip the veggies! Often the challenge of getting people to eat vegetables can be met through new and unexpected recipes. The same people who say that they do not eat salads or vegetables might just find themselves compelled to try a delicious side dish that their dinner companions are raving about.

Sent to Serve

While disposable plates and utensils may seem like a convenient option, using washable, nondisposable dishes, silverware, and drinking glasses is both welcoming and environmentally friendly. Reusable dishes significantly reduce waste. They communicate a

11 Augustine, *On Christian Teaching*, 117.

care for both the dining experience and stewardship of the earth's resources. Many communities already have dinnerware, serving dishes, drinking glasses, and silverware ready to use, even if they have not been used very often in recent times. Additionally, as discussed above with the Dinner Church liturgy, the cleanup process is part of the worship experience.

Using plates, glasses, and silverware that will last is a value statement. If single-use containers need to be used, then organizers should do some research into compostable materials that can be turned back into soil rather than sent to a landfill. While practical considerations might make single-use dishes and utensils a reality in some cases, it is theologically and socially responsible to be aware of the waste being generated in church gatherings and look for reusable options as much as possible.

Arranging the Space

Your space can be arranged in any configuration, based on availability and the desired atmosphere. Round tables work for meals, as do long tables. Whatever the shape of the table, tables should be thoughtfully placed around the room, ensuring there is space to move in and out from tables and that all diners can see the speakers from their seats. Consideration of table spacing and chair placement becomes especially important when there are mobility needs; it is hospitable to assume there will be multiple people using mobility devices joining the meal and to plan the space accordingly. As Amy Kenny has written about inclusive public spaces, "the structures we have put in place often disable people more than individual bodies do."[12] Seating arrangements and serving plans can unintentionally be sources of exclusion.

As a related consideration, worship might begin and end with participants forming a circle surrounding the tables. Movement like this can be unifying and bring everyone's attention together before

12 Kenny, *My Body is Not a Prayer Request*, 11.

they go to their tables for the meal or when everyone is gathered back together following the meal cleanup. In that case, worship leaders should still be easily visible, either as part of the circle or in the center. Whatever arrangement you choose, think about ways that the seating and worship locations might best express the inclusion and fellowship you and your community hope to share through this meal. While not the most obvious theological statement, theology is indeed communicated in every aspect of the meal. As such, it is worth asking what seating arrangements will help everyone see and feel that they are part of the worship meal.

Because the meal revolves around the celebration of the Lord's Supper, it is also important to think ahead about the table that will be used when the time comes for the eucharistic liturgy, often called "The Great Thanksgiving." What can you use for an altar, and how can Communion be centered both liturgically and spatially? Remember that Dinner Church invites creativity and fresh eyes to see what is already available. A small table, a rolling kitchen island, a workshop bench, one humble table among others; your community likely already has many items that could contribute not just to the space itself but to the meaning of what is happening in that space.

As people arrive, a volunteer greeter can be responsible for saying hello, providing name tags, and then either directing people to last-minute tasks that need to be done or inviting them to a place where they can join a conversation. Those who arrive early might get to work warming up the bread, slicing olives or tomatoes for the salad, laying out tablecloths, setting tables, assembling seasonal wreaths (especially in Advent and Lent), or arranging the decorations. It can also be nice to have some extra hands ready to join in the action in case more tables or place settings need to be set up as more people arrive. If the gathering space does not have clear directions to the bathrooms, a good host should provide that information, as well.

Although this has been mentioned before, please do not overlook the power of a name tag! As a valuable component of hospitality, a name tag ensures that people will be called by their preferred name, while communicating to visitors that they are not alone in their need to know the names and identities of others. Think of it as a primary tool that instantly communicates hospitality, belonging, identity, and unity. This can also be a great station for children or teens to staff, as they introduce themselves and offer warm greetings.

Overall, Dinner Church is full of ways people might serve. Children can set out silverware. People with limited mobility can greet or be ready to start conversations around tables. Teens can fill water pitchers and then water glasses. Adults can plate, slice, or scoop food onto shared platters. In Dinner Church, all are invited to have a role, whether they choose one that easily matches their gifts or stretches their comfort zones. This sense of shared ownership contributes to the meaningfulness of the worship experience and lets people know that they belong and are valued in this holy space.

Finishing Touches

Music sets an important tone for Dinner Church. What songs will be sung, and what will be used for accompaniment? In Dinner Church we show up exactly as we are, bringing our whole selves to worship. What songs does the community collectively know, or what would be simple songs to teach without having to keep track of hymnals or printed sheets of paper? One might consider contemplative songs that encourage reflection through repetition or other songs that have a simple, memorable chorus. Along with guitar or piano accompaniment, instruments as varied as a violin, a shruti box, or light percussion can add warmth and expression to the service.

Just as everyone who attends Dinner Church can take part in setting up and preparing the meal, everyone should also have a role in the cleaning and resetting of the space. The postmeal work is intentionally built into the liturgy; this part of the service can be incredibly formative and worshipful for a community. Have a list of all the jobs that must be done, reserving nothing for the leaders alone. At an appropriate moment in the liturgy, typically following the Prayers of the People and the partaking of the final element of wine or juice, a leader can read off the cleanup list one task at a time, securing volunteers for each role. Care can be taken to ensure there is a variety of ability and experience in each cleanup group so that each task has what it needs to be done well. As one body, participants will shift into service: washing dishes, sweeping floors, wiping counters, taking out trash, and packaging leftovers. In the work of serving each other, the assembly will find connection and time for informal conversation, bringing energy and new life to the group. When facilitated well, this work can be completed in about twenty minutes and the group can return to the worship space for dessert, announcements, and a final song that will bring closure to a worship experience that has nourished their whole, holy selves.

Whether there are nine or ninety participants, the model for Dinner Church is flexible. You may find that Dinner Church services start out with lower attendance that grows as the weeks go on and word spreads about the powerful experience. However the worship takes shape, the liturgy and the meal will communicate the value of personal connections, the holiness of worshipping together, and God's great abundance. Through these worship experiences, participants continue to learn about the hungers that exist in and around them, the nourishment that is sought, and the power of the Holy Spirit to connect and engage, unite and restore, feed and share.

DINNER CHURCH RECIPES: POT PIE WITH MASSAGED KALE SALAD AND GRAPES

Meat is not the star of this meal. Although meat, such as chicken or ground beef, can be included, it is both cost efficient and inclusive of dietary restrictions to leave it off the table. While some people might think that they cannot possibly be satisfied by a meatless meal, it is a joy to hear such people share their surprise when they discover otherwise. In this way, Dinner Church can introduce people to new styles of food and approaches to eating, potentially leading to increased openness and creative forms of stewardship in other parts of their lives.

With this recipe, participants will enjoy a veggie pot pie that is delicious and satisfying. The recipe strategy below will make enough for around ten people and can easily be doubled, tripled, quadrupled, etc., based on how many people are expected to attend.

Veggie Pot Pie

Begin by gathering fresh vegetables, including five cloves of garlic, five sticks each of celery and carrots, one large yellow onion, and two pounds of small yellow potatoes. If you have access to fresh rosemary, sage, thyme, or parsley, gather those as well. If not, dried herbs will be fine. Finally, have two cups of vegetable stock, one-third of a cup of flour, one-third of a cup of unsalted butter, one cup of milk or heavy cream, and half a teaspoon each of ground nutmeg, kosher salt, and black pepper. If you are cooking for people who require gluten-free meals, then you might substitute brown rice flour. If your participants include people who are vegan or dairy free, then you can use a butter substitute such as olive oil and an unsweetened, unflavored, nondairy liquid such as oat milk. You can also substitute the dairy with additional stock.

Pot pie is traditionally topped with a crust of some sort. This can be made from pie crust or biscuits, either homemade or store bought. Turning to refrigerated store-bought biscuit packages, for instance, provides a nice option for those who are not keen on baking their own crust; a large scoop of pot pie with a portion of golden biscuit on top makes a very lovely and satisfying meal. Dietary restrictions can be addressed by using gluten-free biscuits or pie crust, or simply by serving the pot pie in an open-faced style with no crust at all.

To prepare the vegetables, wash and trim the celery, then peel and rinse the carrots and potatoes. Chop the celery, carrots, onions, and potatoes into small, bite-sized pieces. You will have about one cup of chopped onions and two cups each chopped carrots, celery, and potatoes. Peel and mince the garlic and finely chop whatever fresh herbs you have.

Melt the butter in a hot Dutch oven or skillet, then add the onion, celery, carrot, and garlic. Sauté for five to six minutes, stirring occasionally. Add the potatoes and stir, sautéing the mixture for five minutes, then add one tablespoon plus one teaspoon of kosher salt and stir well, scraping the bottom of the pot to ensure nothing sticks. Sprinkle the flour over the potato and vegetables and stir continuously for one to two minutes, until you can no longer see any flour and everything is well incorporated. Pour in the vegetable stock and mix, then slowly add the milk, cream, or a combination of half a cup of milk plus half a cup of cream, stirring to combine and ensuring nothing is stuck to the bottom of the pan. Season with several grinds of black pepper, ground nutmeg, and chopped or dried herbs, mixing to combine. Allow the mixture to simmer together, stirring occasionally and scraping the bottom of the pot, for fifteen to twenty minutes, depending on the size of the potatoes.

The pot pie will be served in a 13×9 casserole dish. While the mixture simmers, preheat the oven to 375 degrees and grease your casserole dish so the pot pie will come out as easily as possible. After fifteen to twenty minutes, taste the potato mixture, ensuring potatoes and vegetables are fully softened, yet still holding their shape. You don't want them to be mushy (overcooked) or crunchy (undercooked)! Adjust any seasonings as desired, until the mixture tastes delicious to you. The mixture should hold together well at this point—saucy, but not runny. If, after stirring, it seems too thick with not enough sauce, simply pour a bit more vegetable broth into the pot and mix it in. If the sauce seems too runny, allow the mixture to continue simmering; it will thicken up in a few more minutes.

Pour the mixture into the prepared casserole dish and smooth the top with a rubber spatula. If using biscuits or pie crust, lay the dough over the top. If you are using biscuits, split each full biscuit in half horizontally—full, thick biscuits will not cook well—and lay each thin biscuit half over the mixture, creating a crust with very little overlap and as much coverage as possible.

The dish now goes into the hot oven and will stay there until your biscuits or pie crust are golden brown, around ten to fifteen minutes, although you should keep the casserole in the oven until the crust is completely golden.

Kale Salad with a Side of Grapes

The salad can be made while the pot pie bakes. For this recipe, use either curly green kale or lacinato (also called dinosaur or Tuscan) kale. Strip the leafy kale greens from their thick stems by sliding your fingers up the stack. Discard the stems. Wash the leaves well, then lay them on a cutting board and slice them into strips about a half-inch wide.

Add the pile of kale ribbons to a large bowl, then prepare a homemade dressing. This is easily scalable based on how much kale is being served. One head of kale yields four to six servings. If you are cooking for ten people, then two hearty heads of kale will be a good starting point.

Two heads of kale will need about one-third of a cup of dressing. Add a quarter of a cup of mayonnaise to a large glass measuring cup, small bowl, or wide-mouthed jar. Sprinkle in one-fourth of a teaspoon of kosher salt and half a teaspoon of garlic powder, then add several grinds of black pepper. Pour three tablespoons of olive oil and two tablespoons of apple cider vinegar into the mix, along with the juice of one lemon (about two tablespoons). Mix the ingredients well, then pour over the kale ribbons. Grate around one-fourth of a cup of fresh parmesan cheese directly into the kale and dressing mixture.

For a vegan dressing, simply omit the mayonnaise and cheese, increasing the quantity of olive oil to one-fourth of a cup and the vinegar to three tablespoons. You can add two tablespoons of nutritional yeast to the mixture, if desired.

With thoroughly washed hands, immerse them directly into the bowl. The kale is about to get a massage! This is a magical little technique that softens the fibrous leaves, making them tender and delicious. If you have ever heard people say that they hate kale, then they probably had never had it prepared like this. While there are some who enjoy raw kale, most of us need to show our kale a little tenderness first.

The goal here is to massage the dressing into the kale leaves for two to three minutes. Really rub the leaves well to distribute the dressing. Once the massage is complete, you can fluff up the salad, drizzling it with a little more lemon juice (to taste) and sprinkling a bit more freshly grated parmesan on top, if cheese is being included.

Finally, wash a couple pounds of fresh grapes well. Any color of grapes will work with this meal, although seedless grapes are a must, and red or purple grapes create the most balanced flavor profile. Place them in serving bowls, ready to be enjoyed.

Serving "family-style"—that is, using large containers of food that get passed around or dished out at the table—is recommended, as it brings an increased level of intimacy and connection. During table setup, make sure every table has the necessary serving utensils and potholders. At the appropriate moment in the service, you can have designated volunteers come to a kitchen window or counter to collect their meal elements. Each table should receive their own bowl of salad, bowl of grapes, and a warm casserole dish of veggie pot pie.

CONCLUSION: THE EXPERIENCE OF DINNER CHURCH

From the dinner that two grieving disciples shared with the risen Christ along the road to Emmaus to the gathering around casserole dishes and salad bowls that Dinner Church participants share within a celebration of the Lord's Supper, meals continue to reveal the grace, abundance, joy, and blessings of God for us.

Sunday morning services of Holy Communion already share this good news directly. Dinner Church is not somehow a "Eucharist Plus" experience or a more special way to share the sacrament. Every Eucharist is a meal that reveals Christ. Dinner Church does, however, invite people to live into Christ's promises and presence in ways that they might not have imagined before. It slows down, stretches, and expands the experience of unity, fellowship, nourishment, and grace that Holy Communion offers. Combining many of the food ministries that this book has discussed—Eucharist, community meals, care for neighbors, awareness of the food systems around us, and food vocations within our communities—Dinner Church highlights the many ways that the New Testament is a meal and the abundance of God is revealed to us through the gift of food.

CONVERSATION AROUND THE TABLE

1. Why do you think Jesus's surprised followers on the road to Emmaus did not recognize Jesus until they were eating with him? Why would eating with Jesus reveal things that we might not otherwise understand or experience? What features of Dinner Church might reveal new things to you?
2. What role does a friendly atmosphere play in how a meal is experienced? What kinds of decorations, centerpieces, dishes, and silverware really let you know that someone cares about you? What creative ways might your faith community have to show people that they are welcomed and cared for? Take time to explore the various cabinets and closets around your building, pulling out various elements you can imagine being used in a Dinner Church setting. You may be surprised by what is already on hand!
3. Are you someone who would prefer to help with setting up a meal, cleaning up afterward, or making sure that good conversation is happening? If you are reading this in a group, tell your discussion partners why you prefer that role.
4. Why is showing consideration for allergies and dietary needs a theological issue? What are some ways that your

community shows care for dietary restrictions? What experiences might have gone into those practices?

5. The pattern of worship in Dinner Church blesses the bread early in the meal, continues with God's word and prayers, and then blesses the cup later. What do you think are some of the impacts of these adaptations of the traditional eucharistic liturgy?
6. This book is intentionally framed by chapters on Holy Communion and Dinner Church. Reflect on the theological message of this organizational structure. Consider how Holy Communion is an entrance to food theology, and the way that all the concepts of this book come together in the celebration and experience of Dinner Church.

CHAPTER 7

Casting Bread, Casting Imagination

PRAYER

Spirit of holiness and liberation,
Build in us imagination
For feasts of welcome, tables set
For meals that haven't happened yet
Foretastes of the feast to come
Whose flavors are the taste of home.
Amen.

INTRODUCTION: "CAST YOUR BREAD UPON THE WATERS"

Go for it!

Take your ideas, hopes, dreams, energy, and joy about connecting food with God's love in your community and run with them.

Encouraging that kind of brave and faith-filled imagination is exactly what this book has been about. While it is possible that some ideas have spoken specifically to your context, ready to be applied from the page to the kitchen, other outcomes for this book that are less direct are also likely and just as valid. Like a good recipe that invites creative adaptation for cooking up something new, you are welcome to use these chapters as your own recipe strategies for building community and sharing the love of God through the gift of food.

Ecclesiastes invites this spirit of brave food-based imagination when it says, "Cast your bread upon the waters, for after many days you will find it again."[1]

This beautiful and mysterious Bible verse invites faith and courage, even as it names the worries we might have about taking risks. After all, bread cast out upon the waters seems like it would sink or dissolve. It might float away and wash up on some distant shore. It could be eaten by fish or birds. The least likely scenario, it seems, is that this bread would return to us in any kind of useful state. And yet, that is exactly what Ecclesiastes asserts.

Our bread will return to us, probably because it was never ours to begin with, but rather has always been a gift of God. The early Christian believers experienced this connection between generosity, abundance, and God's good providing on the day of Pentecost: "All who believed were together and had all things in common. . . . They broke bread at home and ate their food with glad and generous hearts, praising God and having the goodwill of all the people."[2] The disciples experienced the transformative reality that generosity leads to more rather than less. Later in the book of Acts, Paul described receiving precisely that message from the risen Christ, who told him, "It is more blessed to give than to receive."[3] Without turning this verse into a contest between the relative merits of giving and receiving, this passage suggests that giving connects us to the life of God, whose nature and activity is to give out of pure grace and love.

"Casting our bread upon the waters" is a way of saying, "All right, God, let's try this out and see what happens." Truly, in food theology, as in other parts of life, we find that the triune God keeps showing

---

1 Eccl 11:1 NIV (1984).

2 Acts 2:44–47.

3 Acts 20:35.

up in amazing ways. In the face of the ongoing changes, challenges, and uncertainties around us, this message to trust in God and see what happens next can be a core framework that guides our lives and our communities. We can be brave when it comes to living into and sharing God's love for the world. Just as good cooks learn from both the successes and disappointments that happen in the kitchen, we will learn as we go in our own food theology adventures. We might even discover some serendipitous flavor combinations and meal ideas along the way.

With such a perspective, there is no such thing as failure. Dr. Michael J. Sorrell, President of Paul Quinn College in Dallas, Texas, told a group of educators in 2018 that failure is the first step in creating change, because honesty about what is not working invites people to imagine new solutions.[4] At Paul Quinn College, the risk-taking process included deciding in 2010 to convert its football field into a farm. This plan arose from noticing that this historically Black college was located in a "food desert," that is, a part of the city in which there was not good access to fresh, healthy, and affordable food. Starting the farm would also address the problem of student debt by increasing work-study opportunities. Building on the school's core value of "WE over me,"[5] the WE Over Me Farm has indeed become an important resource for Paul Quinn College and the Dallas area for teaching, financial aid, public health, and community outreach.[6]

Similarly, students in a 2023 food theology class at Wartburg Theological Seminary found that their final projects brought them many rewarding experiences. The projects ranged from lesson plans and worship services that focused on how food shares God's love

---

4 Michael J. Sorrell, "WE Over Me: From College to Movement," keynote speech, SXSW EDU conference, Austin, TX, March 6, 2018, https://www.youtube.com/watch?v=snE6nBlwSxY&t=14s.

5 "The Quinnite Culture," Paul Quinn, accessed August 2024, https://paulquinn.edu/the-quinnite-culture/.

6 WE Over Me Farm, Paul Quinn College, accessed August 2024, https://paulquinn.edu/we-me-farm/.

to starting church gardens, raising plants to give to food pantries, considering the experience of the Eucharist in the United States Army combat field, and connecting neighbors with local resources to address hunger. Presenting to the class as students were preparing their final projects, guest speaker Pastor Elisabeth Himmelman described the many ways that food conveys God's blessings by saying, "Food theology moves from getting people to eat to making sure people are fed, which includes body and soul," while "help[ing] a congregation focus on abundance."[7] When it came to trying something new, the students' imaginations came to fruition as they demonstrated the many positive effects that can come from connecting food and faith.

While it remains true that failure is scary, food costs money, and gardens take time, Scripture encourages us to cast our bread on the waters and trust that God's blessings will return to us. Failure is data and mistakes in the kitchen are teaching moments. The apostle Paul shared his own surprising experience of God's grace among the church in Corinth: "I planted, Apollos watered, but God gave the growth. . . . For we are God's servants, working together; you are God's field, God's building."[8]

Seed, water, fields, buildings: the Bible gives so many ways to describe God's work in and among us! Some of us will plant seeds of imagination for nourishing faith. Some will literally plant seeds that grow into food to share with neighbors. Others will water the seeds, organize meetings, raise funds, set tables, cook food, share conversation, do dishes, take notes about what went well and what could be improved, and imagine what might come next. We are fields planted and held together by the Holy Spirit. We are buildings and community centers, living stones whose foundation is Jesus Christ.[9]

---

7 Elisabeth Pynn Himmelman, guest lecture, Wartburg Theological Seminary, Dubuque, IA, April 28, 2023.

8 1 Cor 3:6, 9.

9 See 1 Cor 3:11 and 1 Pet 2:4–5.

With so many ways to think about how we relate to food, faith, community, and the gospel of Jesus Christ, you might ask yourself which images capture your attention as you think about food theology where you are. The image of planting and gardening inspires us to imagine things coming into existence that have not yet been planted, to enjoy the feel of getting our hands dirty, and to know from Genesis 2 that immersing ourselves in the life of this world is what God created us to do. Images of fields, buildings, and living stones invite us to think of the places we gather, made holy not by the physical space itself but by the beloved people we meet and Jesus's promise that "where two or three are gathered in my name, I am there among them."[10]

Take whatever image that energizes you and run with it. Cast your bread on the waters. Try something new. Dare to fail, because we cannot truly fail when we learn something new. Pay attention to what God sends back to you. The humblest efforts lead to great rewards.

Indeed, one of the most enduring things the Reformer Martin Luther ever wrote is about the value of stepping out in faith and trusting God to turn it into something beautiful, an observation that includes a healthy serving of what we have been describing as food theology. Defending his teaching that Christian life is not about escaping imperfection but about God transforming the deepest mixed-up realities of our lives, Luther turned to Jesus's parable: "The kingdom of heaven is like yeast that a woman took and mixed in with three measures of flour until all of it was leavened."[11] Inviting people to trust God to lead us into nourishing paths, Luther wrote,

> The new leaven is the faith and grace of the Spirit. It does not leaven the whole lump at once but gently, and gradually, we become like this new leaven and eventually, a bread of God. This life, therefore, is not godliness but the process of becoming godly, not health but getting well, not being but becoming, not rest but

---

10 Matt 18:20.

11 Matt 13:33.

> exercise. We are not now what we shall be, but we are on the way. The process is not yet finished, but it is actively going on. This is not the goal but it is the right road. At present, everything does not gleam and sparkle, but everything is being cleansed.[12]

As full of timely encouragement as when they were written over five hundred years ago, Luther's words assure us that the Holy Spirit is providing the growth, guiding us in faith, creating goodness where we might least expect it, and turning our very lives into "a bread of God."

REAL-LIFE RESOURCES: COOKING AND FAITH

Cooking and faith are, at their best, imperfect acts. This is a beautiful and bold concept we can embrace both as humans and as people who spend time in the act of feeding. If we wait to believe, wait to implement ideas, wait to create something new with what we have on hand, then we will miss out on paying attention to what is around us and engaging with what is already in front of us.

Conditions are often not "just right" to begin cooking a meal; we are people with lives filled with busyness, packed calendars, local and global concerns, people to care for, things to get done, and varying access to fresh food. And so fast food and rushed, shallow connections fill the gap, acting as temporary fixes for our harried lives. But good, nourishing things created by God and tended by our own selves can come from anywhere: great meals are made all over the world on just a sliver of counter space, on a lap, by a fire, on the street. Meaningful, life-giving connection can come from intentional time spent with another person, however momentary it may be. It's not certainty or perfection that matters or makes a difference in the act of nourishment; it is the act itself, and the

---

12 LW 32:24.

sustenance that follows. What miracles we get to enact each day when we see what is in front of us and use it to make something that nourishes us fully!

Wherever we start, with whatever we have, there are a few best practices that, combined with the reflection questions offered throughout this book, can help you as you cast your bread upon the water. God works with who we are and what we have as we tend to the hungers in and around us.

Kitchen Tools and Processes

Many websites and guides are dedicated to reviewing kitchen tools and products. While there are certainly merits to having superior tools to use in food preparation, a perspective of food theology reminds us that the best tools are the tools that we have on hand. A good, clean cutting board and a sharp knife, a skillet you can heat on the stove, a large pot for soup, pasta, and beans—you can do much with these simple items. From there, consider simple things that can make a difference in your cooking and kitchen flow:

- A catch-all bowl, placed just above the cutting board, can help you immensely. Toss all the little bits of unusable items in the bowl as you go, then dump the contents into the compost bin or trash can at the end. This limits your trips to the compost or trash bin, keeps your workspace tidy, and allows the flow of cooking to progress with fewer interruptions.
- If you are trimming vegetables, a second bowl next to the catch-all bowl is a great idea to collect the usable odds and ends as you chop. Tops of celery, peels of carrot, the ends of onions, parsley stems—once you are done trimming the vegetables, all these items can be transferred to a large ziplock bag in the freezer to await a day where you can use them to make stock for soups.

- Set out the things you know you'll need ahead of time. *Mise en place* is a French culinary concept meaning "set up" that reminds us that knowing exactly what we have on hand, and preparing it for use ahead of time, helps our cooking process be smoother and, arguably, more fun because we can stay in the zone of cooking and preparation rather than dashing around the kitchen every few minutes to gather up ingredients and supplies.
- Good lighting makes a big difference in the kitchen. It's harder to cook well when you cannot see well. If you do not have good overhead lighting, consider utilizing task lamps: a desk lamp aimed over your cooking space, a lamp with an exposed light bulb placed on a shelf near the stove, little battery-operated lights from the hardware store stuck to the underside of your upper cabinets, twinkle lights draped in a way that is both brightening and aesthetically pleasing, a headlamp worn while you chop and mix—there are many ways to brighten up the cook space and thus improve your experience of food preparation.
- An electric kettle can be a handy kitchen tool. Having hot water on hand makes the work of bringing water to a boil go more quickly, as you can transfer water from kettle to pot to speed up the process. It also makes the process of preparing chicken, vegetable, or beef stock easier for those who use bouillon cubes or paste.
- Keep your knives sharp. Even if you do not have "fancy knives" and have used the same set since your college days, you can do great work with them provided they are kept sharp and true. Take your regularly used knives to a knife sharpener in your town, or learn how to sharpen them yourself, a couple of times each year. Dull knives are much more dangerous than sharp ones, as the blade can easily slip and cause injury. Dull knives also make the work of food preparation harder and less enjoyable. Wash your knives by hand after each use (avoiding dishwasher use), dry, and

store well so that the blades do not come into contact with other blades or with hard surfaces. A knife block or good magnetic strip can provide helpful storage options.

- Use good salt and know how salty it is. Throughout this book, the salt that is referenced is kosher salt. Different cooks have different salt preferences, but you should not cook with iodized table salt (although this is a great type of salt for baking), as the measurements will not be accurate, and the flavor will not be the best. One tablespoon of table salt, for instance, will be significantly saltier than one tablespoon kosher salt. That said, different brands of kosher salt have different levels of saltiness. Taste your salt and learn how to use it well. This will make a big difference to your cooking.
- Explore different brands of cooking basics such as salt, olive oil, vinegar, and spices. There can be a big difference in the flavor contained in spices bought in your grocery store compared to spices purchased from specialty stores.[13] This is due to freshness, locality, and variety. Similarly, by tasting different olive oils you will be able to identify different flavors and levels of brightness. You do not need to go to a specialty olive oil store to do this (although a visit to a specialty store can certainly be a fun outing!). Just grab a couple different bottles from your local grocery store and consider which flavors you most enjoy. Same goes for vinegars and salt varieties.

Taste and Tweak

One of the best kitchen tools at your disposal is you! Your tastes, your flavor preferences, and your desired textures will all come to play in the kitchen. As you cook, taste often. Taste everything you can

13 One example of a specialty spice store is the online vendor Diaspora Co, which partners directly with global spice farmers to ensure good working conditions, living wages, fresh product, and exceptional flavor.

throughout the cooking process and make it taste good. Is the flavor lacking? The food may need more salt or a splash of an acid such as vinegar or lemon juice. Is it too salty? Wash a potato well, cut it in half and place the cut side down in whatever you are making. Potatoes are salt absorbers, and with twenty or thirty minutes in the oversalted mixture, it will absorb salt, leaving you with a better-balanced dish. Like it spicy? Consider using different varieties of peppers, chili powders, or hot sauces to spice up your food. Burned your bread? No problem. Use a butter knife to gently scrape the surface of the burned loaf. You will be able to scrape off much of the burned matter.

Of course, no recipe, no matter how well followed, will ever turn out 100 percent the same in every single kitchen. This is because there are so many variances. One whole yellow onion typically equals two cups of chopped onion. But onions come in all different sizes and shapes; you may find that you need to use two onions, or just half of one. The same is true for cloves of garlic. One clove of garlic is approximately equal to one teaspoon of minced garlic. Yet garlic cloves can vary dramatically in size, and you may be a garlic lover or someone who likes their garlic in moderation. Know your tastes and be ready to adjust recipes as needed.

Making great food is not hard, but it does take a bit of intention and time, just as developing or adapting a food ministry takes intention and time. Pay good attention to what you already have, listen well to know what hungers are present, bring in the right ingredients and partners, and tend to your creation as well as you can. When problems arise, manage them the best way you know how and bring in people who can help. With steadiness and courage, nourishment will be found.

SIMPLE RECIPES, BIG IMPACTS

As this book concludes, here are a few final recipes that illustrate God's power to use what is simple for the sake of transformation and blessing. These recipes have multiple uses, and each can be thoroughly enjoyed in easy ways: spread on bread, drizzled over meat or pasta, or dipped into with fruit. Having simple strategies such as these will transform a dish, making flavors pop and turning even the most basic meal into a feast.

Whipped Ricotta with Honey

Combine one sixteen-ounce tub of ricotta cheese with two tablespoons of honey and a quarter of a teaspoon of kosher salt in the bowl of a food processor. Blend on high for one minute. If you do not have a food processor, you can make this in a high-powered blender or even by hand in a mixing bowl with a whisk. The result is sweet, creamy ricotta cheese. You can enjoy this on little crostini toasts, made by slicing a baguette into small ovals, spreading each oval with butter or brushing with olive oil, then sprinkling with salt and broiling on low for four minutes. Add a slice of fresh peach or pear with the crostini. Or dip freshly sliced fruit such as strawberries, figs, peaches, or pears directly into the ricotta. Whipped ricotta also makes a delicious spread for crackers layered with salty meats such as prosciutto, or as a spread on sandwiches; spread it on a toasted slice of sourdough bread and sprinkle with zested lemon peel and freshly ground black pepper for a delightful twist. Leftover whipped ricotta can be stored in its original tub in the refrigerator.

Chimichurri

A bold, fresh sauce with roots in Argentina's cuisine, this condiment is an absolute delight drizzled on grilled meats, roasted potatoes, boiled vegetables, or spread on bread. There are many methods for making delicious chimichurri, but the basics are parsley, garlic, oil, salt, black pepper, and sometimes an acid such as vinegar or lemon juice. One way to make this condiment is to take one bunch of parsley, either flat leaf or curly, and roughly remove the leaves from their stems by turning your knife at an angle and scraping the leaves off in one firm motion. Add the parsley to the bowl of a food processor or to a high-speed blender, along with one or two sliced cloves of garlic, one cup of vegetable, corn, or mild extra-virgin olive oil (a neutral flavored oil is well suited to chimichurri), three-fourths of a teaspoon of kosher salt, and a few grinds of black pepper. You can add a good splash of red wine vinegar or lemon juice if you like. Blend on high speed for one minute. The sauce will be slightly chunky and ready to enjoy, with the fresh, herby sauce emboldening and brightening anything you use it on.[14] Store leftover chimichurri in a tightly sealed jar in the refrigerator.

Basil Pesto

There are many ways to make basil pesto. Here is one method: take one cup of basil leaves that have been removed from their stems and add them to the bowl of a food processor or high-speed blender. Add one clove of sliced garlic, half a cup of olive oil, two tablespoons of lemon juice, and half a teaspoon of kosher salt. Chop a quarter of a cup of almonds, then toast in a hot skillet for two to three minutes. Add toasted, chopped nuts to the basil mixture, blending on high speed for one minute. Basil pesto is delightful mixed with cooked pasta (use one tablespoon of pesto along with two teaspoons of hot pasta water for one serving of pasta), as a sandwich spread, a dip for vegetables, or tossed with a fresh salad.

CONCLUSION: GO FOR IT

There is no right way to show up in the kitchen, just as there is no right way to show up in ministry or in our own faith. We come to food and to food ministry directly from the Communion table, where

---

14 This particular strategy of making chimichurri comes from Sergio Panelo, who learned it from his mother, Graciela (Grace) Sidor Panelo, and who shares it generously with his friends. It is shared here with their permission.

the sacraments of bread and wine are poured out into us, connecting us with our neighbors, the earth, and all of creation. Ultimately, the gift of food is a daily, tangible reminder of God's grace that is always ready to meet us, no matter where we are, and inclusive of all that we are. We do not need to be in a church building to encounter the living God; while Holy Communion is an entrance to food theology and to the experience of the triune God in earthly sustenance, the perspective of food theology invites us to pay attention to the presence of God at all times and in all places: in the food that sustains us, the earth that grounds us, the people who surround us.

We live in a broken world where food resources are not equitably distributed, where people go hungry every day, where disordered thinking and experiences with food are part of the reality for many people. Still, within all that brokenness, with every meal we share, every bite we take, every seed we place in the ground, we encounter the proclamation of a God who so deeply loves humanity that food—which feeds, reconciles, unites, and heals—is accessible to us and given to us. From the soil we were formed, and from the soil we are fed, constantly moved to pay attention to all that is present and available to nourish us. As we make use of what is set before us, so too we offer what is set within and around us, trusting that God in Christ Jesus, through the Holy Spirit, will take what we have to offer and make it more than enough.

CONVERSATION AROUND THE TABLE

1. As you conclude this book, what ideas have resonated with you? What will be your favorite takeaway?
2. What cooking or eating practices do you want to try in your community? Are there any practices that you have already incorporated?
3. What questions do you continue to have? Who would be a good conversation partner for these questions?

4. How will you continue to "cast your bread upon the waters?" What might get in the way of starting something new? What is exciting about looking ahead?
5. Each chapter has started with an original table prayer. If you are interested in writing your own table prayers for personal or shared settings, you might begin by pondering these questions: What do you want to tell God and ask God for in your prayer? What do you want to give thanks for? What biblical or contextual images do you want to include?

Recipes

While the narrative recipes included in each chapter offer a great way to jump into cooking and hone your kitchen confidence, you may prefer a more structured recipe to work with. The recipes below are for you to use, adapt, and tweak to your own tastes: consider them a starting point for your own culinary adventures!

CHAPTER 1: INVITATION TO FOOD THEOLOGY

Reimagining Leftovers with Frittata, Nachos, and Sliders

FRITTATA

One frittata results in 8 wedges.

Ingredients

- Whatever leftovers you have and would enjoy in combination; approximately 1½ to 2½ cups in total
  - Cook any raw ingredients prior to beginning the frittata
    - Cook vegetables until tender
    - Cook meat all the way through
- 7 eggs, beaten
- Approx. 2–4 tbsp milk or cream (omit for dairy free)
- ½ tsp kosher salt
- 4 grinds of black pepper (approx. a pinch)
- ¼ tsp Dijon mustard
- Nonstick cooking spray or 1 tbsp butter, for greasing the skillet

Directions

1. Preheat oven to 350°F and warm a medium, oven-proof, nonstick or cast-iron skillet on the stovetop over medium heat.
2. Combine beaten eggs with salt, black pepper, Dijon mustard, and milk or heavy cream. Mix well.
3. Add the extra frittata ingredients to the bowl with the eggs and mix well.
4. Once the skillet is hot, spray with nonstick cooking spray or add butter and allow to melt and coat the pan, ensuring the bottom and sides are well greased. Pour the contents of the bowl into the skillet, using a rubber spatula to mix, then smooth the mixture out.
5. As the skillet stays over heat, the egg mixture will begin to set along the edges. Use your spatula to gently pull back the sides and tilt the skillet so that runny ingredients come in to fill the space along the side of the skillet. Do not scrape anything off the bottom of the skillet.
6. After 5–6 minutes, the sides should be firm, and the top should still be runny.
7. Transfer the skillet to the oven and allow to bake for 8–10 minutes. The top should be set with minimal to no browning on the top.
8. Use an oven mitt to safely remove the skillet from the oven. Allow to cool on the counter for a couple minutes, then slide the frittata from the skillet to a cutting board and slice into wedges.

Recipe Notes

- Frittata can be served hot, cold, or at room temperature.
- From start to finish, this meal won't take longer than 30 minutes. It should also clear out multiple storage containers and unfinished items in your refrigerator!

NACHO TOPPING OR SLIDER PATTIES

Ingredients

- Approximately 3 cups of a mixture of leftovers or fridge scraps, heated through in a skillet and seasoned to your liking
    - Cook any raw ingredients prior to beginning the following steps
        - Cook vegetables until tender
        - Cook meat all the way through
- For nachos:
    - Chips
    - Grated cheese
    - Toppings such as green onion, sliced black olives, sour cream, avocado, or salsa
- For sliders
    - 4 cups cold, previously cooked rice or quinoa
    - 4 eggs, beaten
    - 2 handfuls of nuts, chopped, such as walnuts, almonds, or cashews
    - Neutral oil
    - Slider buns, small rolls, lettuce, or any toppings as desired (see Recipe Notes)

Directions

To make nachos:

1. Heat oven to 350°F.
2. Prepare a baking sheet with a silicone mat or layer of aluminum foil sprayed with nonstick cooking spray.
3. Spread a layer of tortilla chips on the baking sheet and sprinkle with freshly grated cheese.
4. Place baking sheet in the oven for 5–6 minutes, until cheese is melted and chips are warmed.

5. Remove from oven and spread the heated mixture of left-overs over the bed of cheesy chips. Top with any toppings you like.

To make sliders:

1. Transfer heated mixture to a large bowl and add cold rice and chopped nuts.
2. Taste the mixture, adjusting any seasonings, then add beaten eggs. Mix well.
3. Refrigerate for at least 30 minutes.
4. Over medium heat, warm a thick coating of neutral-tasting oil in the same large skillet you cooked the mixture in and shape small handfuls of the mixture into balls, placing a palmful in your hand and squeezing tightly.
5. Place each ball in the hot oil. Once the pan is filled (leaving 2–3 inches of space between each ball), use your hard spatula to gently flatten the balls and allow to fully brown on one side for about 5 minutes. Don't flip the patties too early, or they'll fall apart.
6. Once fully browned, flip the patty, then do the same on the other side, adding more oil if the pan dries out, and scooping out any chunks of mixture that stay behind so that it doesn't burn. Continue until all the mixture has been fried up into little patties.
7. Serve the sliders on little buns or over a bed of lettuce, along with desired toppings.

Recipe Notes

- Cooled, leftover slider patties will keep well in the refrigerator for a couple days.
- To reheat, place on a baking sheet in a hot oven and bake until warmed through.

- Slider toppings could include:
  - Classic burger: American cheese, mayonnaise/ketchup/mustard, pickle, red onion, and iceberg lettuce
  - Smoky: Barbecue sauce, red onion, cheddar cheese
  - Spicy: Hot wing sauce, blue cheese, romaine lettuce
  - Sweet and tangy: Teriyaki sauce, white onion, pineapple
  - Southwestern: Cilantro, avocado, pepperjack cheese

CHAPTER 2: HOLY COMMUNION

Communion Bread Recipes
You will find two recipes here:

- A whole wheat flour Communion bread.
- A gluten-free and vegan Communion bread that, although it has a long ingredient list, does not use a premixed, gluten-free flour, as those mixes often have ingredients that may be allergens or irritants for others, such as eggs, soy, nuts, xanthan gum, etc. While not universally available, the ingredients here should be accessible from a health foods store or online.

Use your knowledge of your community to prepare whichever loaf best suits your needs! Some communities offer two bread options for Holy Communion. If you do that, just remember that you should not prepare gluten-free loaves simultaneously with whole wheat loaves in the same kitchen due to the risk of cross contamination.

Anytime you are preparing gluten- or allergen-free food you must be very careful about the absolute cleanliness of your surfaces, utensils, supplies, and hands. No cross contamination can happen, or your bread will become unsafe for those with severe allergies. When we say that bread is safe for people with allergies to eat, we must mean it and be able to guarantee that it has not come into contact with allergens at any point. This means all equipment must be well cleaned. Do not share cutting boards, knives, and the like that have had gluten or other allergens on them.

Wash equipment, counters, and hands well, dry with a clean towel, and do not touch or have any other foods out while you are working with this gluten-free Communion bread. Avoiding cross contamination is simple, but does require attention so that all can indeed be welcome, and safe, at the holy feast.

One loaf can serve about 30 people at Eucharist. For instance, if your congregation communes 120 people, 4 loaves should be sufficient.

If planning for a bread-baking workshop as outlined in chapter 2, the following supplies will be helpful to have on hand for usage throughout the event:

Supplies

- Parchment paper or silicone baking mat
- Baking sheet
- Large mixing bowl
- Small mixing bowl or measuring glass
- Whisk
- Plastic spatula
- Baking brush (to spread top of loaves with oil)
- Measuring cups: 1 cup, ½ cup, ¼ cup
- Measuring spoons: ¼ tsp, ½ tsp, 1 tsp, 1 tbsp

WHOLE WHEAT COMMUNION BREAD RECIPE

This makes 2 loaves, approximately 6" in diameter each.

Ingredients

- 1 cup whole wheat flour
- ½ cup all-purpose flour
- ½ tsp baking powder
- ½ tsp salt
- 1 tbsp and 1½ tsp molasses
- 1 tbsp and 1½ tsp honey
- 1½ tsp olive oil, plus 1½ tsp for brushing
- ¼ cup and 2 tbsp boiling water, plus additional boiling water, 1 tbsp at a time, as needed

Directions

1. Preheat oven to 400°F. Begin boiling water.
2. In a medium bowl, mix dry ingredients well with a whisk.
3. Slowly pour in oil, gently working the oil into the dry ingredients with a rubber spatula as you pour.
4. Whisk to combine boiling water, honey, and molasses in a large bowl.
5. Add dry ingredients and oil to the wet ingredients bowl.
6. Mix ingredients well with plastic spatula for a couple of minutes until it comes together. Batter will be sticky. If dry, add water 1 tbsp at a time until it comes together well.
7. Divide batter into roughly 2 equal portions.
8. Shape each portion of dough into a ¼" thick round and place on an ungreased baking pan prepared with the parchment paper.
9. Use a knife or the edge of your spatula to score a cross in the center of each loaf, if desired.

10. Bake loaves on the center rack of oven for 10 minutes.
11. Brush the tops of the loaves lightly with oil and emphasize the score of the cross, as it will have receded a bit during baking.
12. Return to oven for 5–6 minutes.
13. Remove from oven and place loaves directly on a cooling rack. Allow to cool completely before use.

Recipe Notes

- High-altitude bakers may require more water in step 6 and less baking time. Experiment and adjust as needed.
- Unused, unconsecrated loaves freeze and defrost well for future use.
- Versions of Communion bread such as this have been made by many denominations over the years. These specific measurements are adapted based on personal experience with a variety of recipes using similar ingredients. This particular recipe results in a hearty, flavorful bite of Communion bread.

GLUTEN-FREE, VEGAN, AND NUT-FREE COMMUNION BREAD RECIPE

This makes 2 loaves, approximately 9" in diameter each.

Ingredients

- ½ cup and 2 tbsp brown rice flour
- ½ cup and 2 tbsp tapioca flour
- ¼ cup teff flour
- 2 tbsp sugar
- ¼ tsp baking soda
- ½ tsp baking powder
- ¼ tsp salt
- 3 tbsp psyllium husks (ground)[1]
- 2 tbsp oil (grapeseed, avocado, or mild olive oil), plus a bit more for the tops of the loaves
- ¼ tsp apple cider vinegar
- 1 cup water

Directions

1. Heat your oven to 350°F and prepare your baking sheets with a layer of parchment paper or a silicone baking mat.
2. Mix dry ingredients well with a whisk, shaping a well in the center for the wet ingredients.
3. Mix wet ingredients together with your whisk, then pour into the well in the center of the dry ingredients bowl.
4. Mix ingredients well with plastic spatula, then allow the mixture to sit for a couple of minutes until it thickens into a thick batter.
5. Divide batter into roughly 2 equal portions and shape into round loaves on the prepared pan.

---

1 Psyllium husks are often sold in the digestive aids section of a natural grocery store or can be purchased online.

6. Score the loaves with a cross, if desired.
7. Brush the tops of the loaves lightly with oil.
8. Put in oven for 12 minutes.
9. Remove baking sheets from oven. Turn up oven temperature to 400°F.
10. Again, lightly brush loaves with oil and rescore the cross.
11. Return baking pans to oven and bake for an additional 12 minutes.
12. Remove from oven and place loaves directly on cooling rack.
13. Allow to cool completely before use.

Recipe Notes

- High-altitude bakers may require lower heat and less baking time. Experiment and adapt as necessary.
- Unused, unconsecrated loaves freeze and defrost well for future use.
- Defrosting at room temperature is recommended for best texture and flavor.
- If you cannot find teff flour, another gluten-free flour can be substituted. We recommend gluten-free oat flour for the best flavor.
- This recipe was originally developed by Rev. Tami Groth and is used here with permission.

CHAPTER 3: COMMUNITY MEALS

Perfect pasta, simple marinara sauce, savory meatballs, crunchy garlic bread

PERFECT PASTA

Makes 1 lb. of pasta, enough for 3–6 servings.

Ingredients

- Water to fill pot, approx. 4–6 quarts
- 1 tbs kosher salt
- 1 lb. dried pasta of your choice
- Optional toppings, as desired (see Recipe Notes)

Directions

1. Bring 4–6 quarts of water, plus kosher salt, to a boil in a large pot.
2. Add dried pasta once the water is pleasantly salty. Stir well.
3. Allow pasta to gently boil for 1 minute less than the package recommends, stirring occasionally.
4. When the timer goes off, test a noodle by biting it in half. A perfectly cooked noodle should have a faint white line in the middle and a nice firmness, but it should not be crunchy. Return to boil for 1–2 minutes if it is too firm, then test again.
5. Scoop out 2 cups of your salty pasta water and drain off the rest.
6. Top the pasta however you like, using your reserved pasta water to create a sauce, thin out a sauce, or add more flavor down the line.

Recipe Notes

- Possible toppings include:
  - Melted butter, sprinkled salt, ground black pepper, and a grating of parmesan cheese.
  - Marinara sauce and meatballs.
  - Pesto, from chapter 7.
- Any variety of pasta can be used here, including gluten-free pasta made from beans or rice.
- The amount of salt you should add to the water will vary. By tasting the water as it warms, you will learn your preference for how much salt to add. The water should taste pleasantly salty, but not harshly salty.
- Salting pasta water is a forgiving process: if the water gets too salty, ladle some out and add more fresh, unsalted water.

SIMPLE MARINARA SAUCE

Makes a large pot of sauce, enough for 15–20 servings of pasta.

Ingredients

- 8 cloves of garlic, peeled and minced (approx. 8 tsp)
- 4 tbsp olive oil
- 1 pinch crushed red pepper
- 3 28 oz. cans of crushed tomatoes
- 2 14.5 oz. cans of diced tomatoes
- 1 tbsp kosher salt
- 1 tbsp dried oregano
- 2 tsp dried basil
- 8 grinds of black pepper (approx.⅛ tsp)
- Optional: rind of parmesan cheese, ¼ cup red wine

Directions

1. Heat a large pot over medium low heat.
2. Once warm, pour olive oil in to thinly coat the bottom of the pot. Heat, then add minced garlic. Stir with a wooden spoon.
3. Add in a pinch of crushed red pepper flakes, more if you prefer a spicy sauce. Stir.
4. Allow your garlic to completely soften and become fragrant but not brown; 2–3 minutes, stirring often.
5. Garlic burns quickly. Keep an eye on it as it toasts in the olive oil and be sure to move to the next step as the minced garlic is just beginning to turn golden. If the garlic turns brown at all, it is burned, and you will need to throw out the garlic and olive oil and start over, as there is no recovery from burned garlic.
6. Add crushed tomatoes to the pot followed by diced tomatoes. Stir well to combine.
7. Add spices: salt, oregano, basil, black pepper. Stir to combine.

8. Optional: Add a rind from an old block of parmesan cheese. The rind of parmesan cheese will melt into the sauce, adding a depth of flavor without becoming a cheesy sauce. You can also add a few glugs of red wine, stirring well to combine, for a depth of flavor. The alcohol will evaporate out of the simmering sauce as it cooks.
9. Allow pot contents to come to a gentle bubble, then reduce heat to low.
10. Cover, then allow sauce to simmer for as little as 30 minutes and as long as 5 hours with occasional stirring.
11. Taste and adjust spices and salt, as needed.
12. If you added a parmesan rind, it may melt entirely into the sauce, or part of it may remain. If any part of the rind remains, remove it prior to serving. This can be added to your food waste bin.

Recipe Notes

- This marinara sauce can be served over any type of pasta or over the Savory Meatballs.
- If preparing pasta, rigatoni, spaghetti, or bucatini are especially good matches. Set your pot of pasta water to boil around during step 9, above, approximately 20 minutes prior to the time you plan to eat.
- Sauce can be ladled directly onto individual bowls of pasta or pasta can be added directly into the sauce pot for serving.
- Sauce can be cooled, then chilled for leftovers or frozen on its own for up to 6 months. Defrost and reheat in a saucepan for use later on.
- For a sweeter sauce, add 1 tsp white or cane sugar.
- A pinch of baking soda can be added to the sauce to reduce acidity, as needed.

SAVORY MEATBALLS

Makes 30–40 meatballs, 1.5" in diameter.

Ingredients

- 1 yellow onion, well chopped
- 4 cloves garlic, finely minced
- 2 tbsp olive oil
- 1 lb. ground beef, 10–15 percent fat
- 1 lb. ground pork
- ½ cup breadcrumbs (regular or gluten free)
- ¾ cup milk
- ½ cup chopped flat-leaf parsley (or 1 tbsp dried parsley)
- ¼ tsp hot sauce
- 1 tsp Worcestershire sauce
- ½ tsp Dijon mustard
- 2 eggs, mixed
- 1 tbsp dried oregano
- 2 tsp kosher salt
- 16 grinds of black pepper (approx. ¼ tsp)
- ¼ cup parmesan cheese or nutritional yeast

Directions

1. With a hot skillet set over medium heat, sauté onion in olive oil for around 6 minutes then add garlic cloves. Stir until fragrant; approximately 1–2 minutes.
2. Remove the pan from heat and allow garlic and onion to cool.
3. Add your ground meat to a large mixing bowl.
4. Place breadcrumbs in a separate small bowl. Add milk, stir, and allow to sit for 3–5 minutes so that the breadcrumbs absorb the milk.
5. Add parsley, hot sauce, mustard, Worcestershire sauce, eggs, oregano, kosher salt, black pepper, and nutritional

yeast or parmesan cheese to the meat in the large mixing bowl and stir to combine.

6. Add cooled sautéed onions and garlic and soaked breadcrumbs to the meat mixture.
7. Using very clean hands, mix ingredients together well. Allow the mixture sit in the fridge for anywhere from 30 minutes to overnight.
8. When you are ready to roll the mixture into meatballs, preheat oven to 350°F and prepare two baking sheets with silicone mats or aluminum foil with a coating of nonstick cooking spray, and set near a large mixing bowl.
9. Roll the meat mixture into small balls (around golf ball size, approx. 1.5" in diameter) and lay them in rows on the prepared baking sheets. Alternately, you can use a cookie scooper to scoop and make the balls.
10. If you're using your hands and the meat mixture is too sticky, wash your hands and leave them a little wet: damp hands will keep the mixture from sticking to you.
11. Each baking tray can have its own rack in the oven, switching spots halfway through the cooking time.
12. Bake meatballs for twenty to thirty minutes. They will be ready when you see caramelization, or browning, on the outside and an inside that is cooked through but still moist.

Recipe Notes

- You can easily make this a half, double, or triple batch, freezing unused portions for next time.
- To freeze, line up the rolled, uncooked balls on a baking sheet and place them in the freezer for several hours.
- Once the meatballs are frozen through, move them to a plastic freezer bag or container and keep frozen until needed.
- Frozen meatballs can be placed on a baking sheet to defrost in the refrigerator, then baked as directed above.

- Breadcrumbs can be store bought or homemade.
- If you prefer a lower fat version of the meatballs, you can substitute the pound of ground pork for an additional pound of ground beef, or substitute it with ground bison or turkey.

CRUNCHY GARLIC BREAD

Serves 4–6.

Ingredients

- 1 loaf of unsliced Italian or French bread, halved lengthwise
- 1 stick unsalted butter, softened (you can also use a stick of salted butter)
- ½ tsp kosher salt (omit if using salted butter)
- 2 tsp dried oregano
- 2 tsp garlic powder
- 1 tsp paprika

Directions

1. Preheat oven to 350°F.
2. Mix together the softened stick of butter along with all seasonings.
3. Spread thickly on each bread half, and place on a baking sheet.
4. Slide baking sheet into the oven and allow to cook 10 minutes.
5. Switch the oven to the low broiler setting and allow the top to crisp up for approximately 2 minutes, keeping a (very) close eye on it so it does not burn.
6. Remove from oven, cool for a minute, then slice into thick chunks.

Recipe Notes

- This recipe comes from Lauri Lisi's kitchen, where garlic bread accompanies every Italian meal she serves. Simple, crunchy, and surprisingly delicious, it's the perfect accompaniment to marinara sauce.

CHAPTER 4: NEVER LEAVE HUNGRY

Chilled lentil salad, hot lentil soup

CHILLED LENTIL SALAD

Serves 10 as a side dish.

Ingredients

- 1 lb. dried brown lentils (approx. 2½ cups), well rinsed
- 6 cups water
- 2–3 tsp kosher salt
- 2 tbsp red wine vinegar
- 1 tbsp olive oil
- Other ingredients, as desired (see Recipe Notes)

Directions

1. Add rinsed lentils to a saucepan. Cover with 6 cups of water and add salt. Stir.
2. Bring the pot to a boil and allow to simmer, uncovered. Simmer for 25–30 minutes, removing from heat once the lentils are soft and taste good to you.
3. Run the cooked lentils under cold water so that they do not continue to cook and get mushy.
4. Drain lentils and toss with red wine vinegar and olive oil. Gently mix, then taste and adjust seasoning as desired.
5. Chill the mixture so that all the ingredients come together and the flavors meld. You can eat your lentil salad cold out of the fridge or at room temperature.

Recipe Notes

- Leftovers will keep in the fridge.
- Once cooled, cooked lentils can be packaged for later use and stored in the fridge.

- Green lentils are also a great match for chilled lentil salad. Refer to the bag for cooking directions, as green lentils typically take longer to cook.
- Lentils can be eaten as is, or dressed up with any of following variations, or however else you might imagine their flavors coming to life. A few possible variations include:
    - ¼ cup feta cheese, ½ cup pitted and sliced kalamata olives, ½ cup halved cherry tomatoes, a handful of sliced spinach, a ½ cup chopped cucumbers, along with 1 tsp of garlic powder and a ½ tsp oregano.
    - 1 cup chopped pickled vegetables or giardiniera and 1/4 cup of thinly sliced red onion.
    - 1/2 cup of cubed cheddar cheese, 1/4 cup each sliced black olives and sliced sundried tomatoes, 1 cup destemmed and thinly sliced lacinato kale leaves, along with 1 tsp of garlic powder and ½ tsp oregano.
    - A dusting of freshly ground parmesan cheese and an extra drizzle of olive oil.

HOT LENTIL SOUP

Serves 10.

Ingredients

- 1 lb. brown lentils (approx. 2½ cups), well rinsed
- 6 cups water
- 2–3 tsp kosher salt, divided
- 5 tbsp olive oil, divided
- 1 large yellow onion, peeled and chopped
- 4 carrots, peeled and chopped
- 4 stalks trimmed celery, chopped
- 4 cloves of garlic, peeled and minced
- Optional: pinch of red pepper
- 12 cups chicken or vegetable stock, or bouillon to make an equivalent amount of stock
- 1 tbsp red wine vinegar
- Other ingredients, as desired (see Recipe Notes)

Directions

1. Add rinsed lentils to a saucepan. Cover with 6 cups water and 2 tsp salt. Stir.
2. Bring the pot to a boil, cover, and allow to simmer for 20 minutes. Lentils will still be a bit crunchy.
3. As the lentils simmer, chop your vegetables into approx. ½" pieces.
4. Heat a soup pot over medium heat and pour 3 tbsp olive oil into the pot.
5. Once warm, add the onion. Stir, sautéing for 5 minutes, then add the carrots and celery to the pot, along with the remaining 2 tbsp olive oil. Salt with 1 tsp kosher salt. Stir and sauté for 5 additional minutes, then add garlic to the hot oil and sauté together for 1 minute.

6. Optional: add a small pinch of crushed red pepper flakes simultaneously with the garlic and allow to toast.
7. Prepare the soup base by adding stock to the sautéed ingredients, and bring it all to a simmer.
8. Once the lentils are done simmering in their own pot, stir in red wine vinegar, then add lentils to the soup pot.
9. Stir, then bring all ingredients to a simmer. Simmer for 10 minutes.
10. Taste and adjust any seasonings to your liking.

Recipe Notes

- This recipe is the basis for other directions you may want to take the lentil soup, or it can be eaten as is. Variations include:
    - Cook rice on the side and, once cooked, add to the final lentil soup.
    - Add diced potatoes to the veggie and garlic mixture, sautéing together for 6 additional minutes. Then, cover with stock and bring to a gentle boil. Potatoes will be cooked in approximately 20 minutes.
    - Add 1 tbsp curry powder following the addition of garlic, stirring for 1 minute, then pour in 1 can of unsweetened coconut milk and 1 cup of vegetable stock.
- Leftover soup can be cooled and refrigerated.

CHAPTER 5: FIELDS AND TABLES

Croutons, roasted chickpeas, herbed vinaigrette, tangy maple dressing, candied nuts

CRISPY CRUNCHY CROUTONS

Results in approx. 4 cups of croutons, enough for 8–10 salads.

Ingredients

- ½ loaf day-old bread, about 5 cups worth
- 1 tbsp olive oil for each cup of bread
- 1 tsp each kosher salt, garlic powder, and paprika
- 2 tsp oregano

Directions

1. Preheat the oven to 400°F. Line a baking sheet with parchment or aluminum foil for easier cleanup.
2. Roughly tear or cube whatever bread you have on hand and spread it out on a rimmed baking sheet.
3. Coat the bread with olive oil and toss.
4. Sprinkle with salt, garlic powder, paprika, and oregano. Toss with a spatula or your clean hands.
5. Place in the center of the oven and toast for 14–16 minutes, removing from oven at the halfway point and flipping each bread chunk with the spatula to allow more even toasting.
6. Remove from oven and allow to cool slightly before adding to salad.

Recipe Notes

- Any kind of bread will work here. You can use sliced sandwich bread, baguette, French or Italian loaf, sourdough, etc.
- Leftover croutons can be placed in a sealed container for later use.

ROASTED CHICKPEAS

Results in approx. 1 ½ cups of roasted chickpeas.

Ingredients

- 2 15 oz. cans chickpeas (also known as garbanzo beans)
- 2 tbsp olive oil
- 1 tsp each kosher salt, garlic powder, paprika, and oregano

Directions

1. Preheat the oven to 400°F.
2. Line the baking sheet with parchment or aluminum foil for easier cleanup.
3. Drain and rinse the chickpeas, then spread out on a rimmed baking sheet.
4. Coat the beans with olive oil and sprinkle with salt and all seasonings. Toss with a spatula or clean hands.
5. Place the baking sheet in the center of the oven and roast for around 30 minutes, removing the baking sheet at the halfway point to gently shake the chickpeas so that they wiggle around for more even crisping.
6. Remove the chickpeas from the oven when they reach desired level of crispiness; around 30 minutes.

Recipe Notes

- You can create this crunchy snack with any spice mixture you want. Consider trying a combination of cumin, garlic powder, chili powder, and salt, or trying curry powder with salt.
- Roasted chickpeas are delicious when added to salads or eaten on their own as a high-protein snack.
- Leftover chickpeas can be stored in an airtight container in the refrigerator.

HERBED VINAIGRETTE

Results in approx. 1 cup of salad dressing.

Ingredients

- 1 tsp Dijon mustard
- 1 tsp of each kosher salt, dried basil, powdered garlic, dried parsley, powdered onion, and white sugar
- 1 tbsp dried oregano
- ⅓ cup red wine vinegar
- ⅔ cup olive oil

Directions

1. Begin with a mason jar or other jar with a well-fitting lid.
2. Add Dijon mustard and all spices, including salt and sugar.
3. Pour in red wine vinegar. Mix well, using a fork.
4. Slowly drizzle in olive oil, briskly mixing with the fork as you go.
5. Dress each serving of salad with approximately 1 tbsp of dressing.

Recipe Notes

- Dressing can be stored in the jar in the fridge.
- The olive oil will solidify in the fridge. Simply leave out on the counter to allow the oil to come to room temperature again and shake the jar well.

TANGY MAPLE DRESSING

Results in approx. 1 cup of salad dressing.

Ingredients

- 1 tsp Dijon or whole grain mustard
- ¼ cup maple syrup
- 1 tsp kosher salt
- 8 twists freshly ground black pepper
- ⅓ cup white wine vinegar
- ⅔ cup olive oil

Directions

1. Begin with a mason jar or other jar with a well-fitting lid.
2. Add mustard, maple syrup, salt, and pepper.
3. Pour in white wine vinegar. Mix well, using a fork.
4. Slowly drizzle in olive oil, briskly mixing with the fork as you go.
5. Dress each serving of salad with approximately one tablespoon dressing.

Recipe Notes

- Apple cider vinegar is a delightful substitute for white wine vinegar.
- Dressing can be stored in the jar in the fridge. Shake well before serving again.
- The olive oil will solidify in the fridge. Simply leave out on the counter to allow the oil to come to room temperature again and shake the jar well.

CANDIED NUTS

Results in approx. 1 cup of candied nuts.

Ingredients

- 1 cup roughly chopped nuts (almonds, walnuts, pecans, or cashews)
- 1 tbsp water
- 2 tbsp sugar
- ¼ tsp kosher salt

Directions

1. Warm a skillet over low heat.
2. Prepare a layer of parchment paper or a silicone mat on the counter.
3. Add chopped nuts and allow to lightly toast, gently and frequently shaking the skillet back and forth (or stirring with a spatula) so that the nuts don't burn.
4. Toast for 3 minutes.
5. Add water, sugar, and salt, stirring well with a spatula.
6. Allow sugar to dissolve and thoroughly coat the nuts.
7. Once the nuts have reached desired toastiness—about 2 minutes—spread the sticky mixture on the prepared surface.
8. Allow nuts to cool to the touch, then break up any clusters with clean hands or a light smack from the bottom of a flat skillet or pan.

Recipe Notes

- Candied nuts can be added directly to salads or eaten on their own.

CHAPTER 6: DINNER CHURCH

Veggie pot pie, massaged kale salad

VEGGIE POT PIE

Makes one 13×9" casserole dish, enough for 6–8 servings.

Ingredients

- ⅓ cup unsalted butter (sub olive oil for vegan)
- 1 large yellow onion, chopped
- 5 sticks each of celery and peeled carrots, both chopped
- 5 cloves garlic, peeled and minced
- 2 lb. small yellow potatoes, skin on and cubed into pieces around ½ inch wide
- 1 tbsp and 1 tsp Kosher salt
- ⅓ cup flour (sub. brown rice flour to make gluten free)
- 2 cups vegetable stock
- 1 cup whole milk, or ½ cup heavy cream and ½ cup whole milk for richer flavor (sub. same amount vegetable broth, or unsweetened, unflavored oat milk for vegan)
- 3 tbsp fresh herbs, such as rosemary, sage, thyme, or parsley, finely chopped or 1 tbsp combination of dried herbs
- ½ tsp ground nutmeg
- 8 grinds of black pepper (approx. ¼ tsp)
- Refrigerated biscuit dough or pie crust (see Recipe Notes for gluten-free options)

Directions

1. Heat a large skillet or Dutch oven over medium heat.
2. Melt butter, then add onion. Sauté for 1 minute, then add carrots, celery, and garlic. Sauté 5–6 minutes, stirring occasionally.

3. Add potatoes to the vegetable mixture. Allow to sauté together for 5 minutes, then sprinkle in kosher salt and stir well, scraping the bottom to ensure nothing sticks.
4. Sprinkle flour over the potato and vegetables and stir continuously for 1–2 minutes, until you can no longer see any flour and everything is well incorporated.
5. Pour in vegetable stock and mix together, then slowly add the milk or milk/cream mix, stirring to combine and ensuring nothing is stuck to the bottom of the pan.
6. Season with black pepper, ground nutmeg, and chopped or dried herbs, mixing to combine.
7. Allow the mixture to simmer together, stirring occasionally and scraping the bottom of the pan for 15–20 minutes, depending on the size of the potatoes.
8. Preheat oven to 375°F.
9. Grease a 13×9" casserole dish.
10. Taste the mixture, ensuring potatoes and vegetables are fully softened, yet still holding their shape. You don't want them to be mushy (overcooked) or crunchy (undercooked)! Adjust seasoning as desired.
11. The mixture should hold together well at this point: saucy, but not runny. If, after stirring, it seems too thick, simply pour a bit more vegetable broth into the pan and mix. If the sauce seems too runny, allow the mixture to continue simmering; it will thicken up in a few more minutes.
12. Pour the mixture into the prepared casserole dish and smooth the top with a rubber spatula. If using biscuits or pie crust, lay the dough over the top.
13. If you are using biscuits, split each full biscuit in half horizontally—full, thick biscuits will not cook well—and lay each thin biscuit half over the mixture, creating a crust with very little overlap and as much coverage as possible.
14. Insert casserole dish into the hot oven and cook until the crust is evenly golden brown; 10–15 minutes.

Recipe Notes

- For gluten free: omit biscuits and serve as a thick stew, or use a gluten-free product such as Sweet Loren Puff Pastry (found in refrigerated section of the grocery store) or Red Lobster Gluten Free Biscuit Mix.
- If a protein is desired, use half the amount of potatoes and kosher salt listed in the ingredients and add 1–2 cups of chopped or shredded cooked chicken during step 10.

MASSAGED KALE SALAD

Serves 10 people as a side dish.

Ingredients

- 2 heads of kale, either curly green or lacinato varieties
- ¼ cup mayonnaise
- ¼ tsp kosher salt
- ½ tsp garlic powder
- 4 grinds of black pepper (approx. ⅛ tsp)
- 3 tbsp olive oil
- 2 tbsp apple cider vinegar
- 1 lemon, juiced, with 1 tsp reserved for final step
- ¼ cup fresh parmesan cheese, with additional 2 tbsp reserved for final step

Directions

1. Strip the leafy kale greens from their thick stems by sliding your fingers up the stalk. Discard stems and wash the leaves well.
2. Lay on a cutting board and slice kale leaves into strips about a half-inch wide.
3. Add the kale ribbons to a large bowl, then prepare the homemade dressing.
4. Add mayonnaise to a large glass measuring cup, small bowl, or wide-mouthed jar. Sprinkle in kosher salt and garlic powder, then several grinds of black pepper.
5. Pour olive oil and apple cider vinegar into the mix, as well as the lemon juice.
6. Mix the ingredients well, then pour over the kale ribbons.
7. Grate fresh parmesan cheese and add to the mixing container.
8. Massage kale with thoroughly washed hands for approximately 2–3 minutes, rubbing leaves well to distribute the dressing.

9. Fluff up the salad, drizzling it with a little more lemon juice (to taste) and sprinkling a bit more freshly grated parmesan on top, if cheese is being included.

Recipe Notes

- Prepared salad can be refrigerated in a sealed container for 1 day.
- For a vegan dressing, simply omit the mayonnaise and cheese, increasing the quantity of olive oil to ¼ cup and the vinegar to 3 tbsp. You can add 2 tbsp of nutritional yeast to the mixture, if desired.

CHAPTER 7: CASTING BREAD, CASTING IMAGINATION

Whipped ricotta with honey, chimichurri, basil pesto

WHIPPED RICOTTA WITH HONEY

Ingredients

- 16 oz. whole milk ricotta cheese
- 2 tbsp honey
- ¼ tsp kosher salt

Directions

1. Scoop ricotta into the bowl of a food processor.
2. Add honey and kosher salt.
3. Blend on high speed for 1 minute.

Recipe Notes

- You can also use part-skim ricotta with good results.
- Spread ricotta on bread, crostini, or crackers.
- Dip sliced peaches, pears, figs, or dried apricots.
- Consider the addition of freshly zested lemon peel for a citrus-infused option.

CHIMICHURRI

Ingredients

- 1 head of parsley (approx. 1 cup), leaves removed from stems
- 1–2 cloves garlic, sliced
- 1 cup vegetable, corn, or mild extra-virgin olive oil
- ¾ tsp kosher salt
- A few grinds of black pepper
- A splash of red wine vinegar or lemon juice, if desired

Directions

1. Add all ingredients into the bowl of a food processor or high-speed blender.
2. Blend on high speed for 1 minute.

Recipe Notes

- Chimichurri brightens everything it meets: meat, bread, potatoes, roasted vegetables—all are worthy vehicles for this fresh, herby sauce.
- Vegetable and corn oil both provide a neutral backdrop for the chimichurri flavors to shine through, while olive oil will lend a rich flavor of its own. You can also use a half-cup of neutral oil combined with a half-cup of olive oil.
- This particular strategy of making chimichurri comes from Sergio Panelo, who learned it from his mother, Graciela (Grace) Sidor Panelo, and who shares it generously with his friends. It is shared here with their permission.

BASIL PESTO

Ingredients

- 1 cup basil leaves, removed from stem
- 1 clove garlic, sliced
- ½ cup olive oil
- ½ tsp kosher salt
- 2 tbsp lemon juice
- ¼ cup chopped, toasted almonds or whole, toasted pine nuts

Directions

1. Add all ingredients into the bowl of a food processor or high-speed blender.
2. Blend on high speed for 1 minute.

Recipe Notes

- Basil pesto is delightful mixed with pasta and ¼ cup hot pasta water, as a spread for a sandwich, or a dip for vegetables.
- You can swap out the basil for spinach for equally delicious results. This is a particularly enjoyable swap in the fall, winter, and spring when basil is not in season.

Appendix 1: Dietary Accommodations and Substitutions

Here you will find supplemental materials for the previous chapters. Review this section to learn more about how to accommodate various dietary needs.

Gluten free: For people with celiac disease, it is critical that safe practices are followed. Cutting boards, knives, mixing spoons, towels, etc. must all be clean and uncontaminated with gluten. Gluten-free pastas, breads, crackers, flour, and other products are readily available, and any can be substituted for wheat pasta, bread, flour, etc. that are named in recipes.

Dairy free: Substitute milk or cream with an unsweetened, unflavored, nondairy version such as oat milk (look for a certified gluten-free version) or flax milk. You will want to avoid almond, coconut, or cashew milks in large group meals when you are not sure of potential nut allergies. Omit cheese. There are many nondairy cheeses available, although these are often made from nuts, which again could be problematic for folks with dairy and nut allergies. It may be easiest to simply stay away from recipes requiring cheese. People who are dairy free may also have egg allergies, which eliminates mayonnaise, as well.

Nut free: There are many types of nut allergies, including peanuts, tree nuts, and coconuts. For some people, their nut allergies are potentially fatal. Generally, when cooking for a large group of people with unknown food allergies, it is best to avoid nuts altogether. For some folks with nut allergies, it is not a simple matter of avoiding nuts themselves; it is unsafe for them to have anyone in the room consuming nuts. This includes nut milks and nut-based cheese replacements. Be sure to read labels carefully, especially for desserts, as foods that are processed with nuts are quite ubiquitous and can also be dangerous for folks with severe allergies.

Soy free: Substitute coconut aminos for soy sauce. Avoid soybean, soy milk, soy sauce, and tofu products.

Vegetarian: This means no meat or meat-derived products. Depending on the person, this can include eggs, mayonnaise, or anchovies (which are a common ingredient in some salad dressings).

Vegan: This means no animal products of any kind, including eggs, honey, and dairy products. All the modifications for vegetarians are necessary for a vegan dish, as well as the modifications for dairy free.

There are many other variations of dietary restrictions. Be sure to communicate with people in your context to learn how to safely cook for them.

Appendix 2: Sample Liturgy for an Agape Meal

This sample liturgy provides a model for an Agape meal that you can adapt to suit your context and goals. It is helpful in advance to assign a leading minister and an assisting minister, then recruit up to nine volunteers for other speaking roles. This invitation allows many voices to be heard, enriching the gathering.

Bible readings, poems, or other relevant texts should be selected before the meal that speak to the local setting. An Agape meal that happens during a congregational soup supper, for instance, could include readings about generosity or stories written by those who have struggled with food insecurity. A meal that takes place while teaching youth about Holy Communion might use hymns, poetry, or pictures that focus on the sacrament to spark imagination and discussion. Intercessory prayers have been included here for the gathering to use, but an assembly would be welcome to write its own prayers.

This liturgy has been successfully used in a variety of in-person and online settings. Participants have gathered on laptops and cell phones, in classrooms and fellowship halls, or some combination of the above at the same time. If digital technology is already being used, then videos or other visual media can easily be used to complement the readings to good effect.

The leading minister welcomes people by giving an overview of what will happen, asking for volunteers (if they were not arranged ahead of time), and explaining the process for getting food and eating together. In the following example, people already have their food and will begin eating after the Table Prayer that precedes the readings.

GATHER

Leading Minister: We gather in the light and peace of Jesus Christ our Lord.

People: Thanks be to God.

Assisting Minister: Let us pray: God our creator, you have ordered seed-time and harvest, sunshine and rain. Give to all who work the land fair compensation for the work of their hands. Grant that the people of this and every nation may give thanks to you for food, drink, and all that sustains life; may use with care the land and water from which these good things come; and may honor the laborers who produce them, through your Son, Jesus Christ our Lord.[1]

People: Amen.

CONFESSION AND FORGIVENESS

Reader 1: As we gather for this meal, we acknowledge our need for each other and our need for a nourishing world.

People: Bring your nourishment to us, O God.

Reader 2: We recognize the ways we create excess waste and do not always notice or take proper care of the resources we have.

People: Bring your nourishment to us, O God.

Reader 3: We confess to the injustices of our modern food production system, the harm caused by these inequities, and the hurt that falls disproportionately on communities experiencing racial discrimination throughout the world.

People: Bring your nourishment to us, O God.

Reader 4: We admit how our separation from our food creates separation between us and the land and from your entire, abundant creation.

People: Bring your nourishment to us, O God.

Reader 5: We remember that many in this world are hungry and do not have enough to eat, despite the plentiful abundance of food that is produced globally.

People: Holy and almighty God,
For the sake of your Son, Jesus Christ,

1 Evangelical Lutheran Church in America, *Evangelical Lutheran Worship*, 78.

have mercy on us.
Forgive us, renew us, and lead us,
so that we may delight in your will
and walk in your ways,
to the glory of your holy name. Amen.[2]

Assisting Minister: Like us, Jesus experienced loneliness and grief, joy and thanksgiving. Like us, Jesus hungered and ate with his friends. In his great mercy and love, he gave his life so that we might live reconciled with God, the world, and each other. In his name, your sins are forgiven. Through the Holy Spirit we are cleansed and given power to proclaim the mighty deeds of God who created the mountains and the animals, the streams and the sun, the forests and the plants, and all of humanity.

COMMUNAL FEAST

Leading Minister: Our mealtime conversation today will be based on the following texts [or videos, images, etc.].[3] After these readings, we will spend ten minutes in small groups to discuss what we heard and what resonated with each of us.

Table Prayer

Leader 6: Let us pray: For the bountiful table you prepare for us, God, we give you thanks. Bless our conversation and fellowship. Help us welcome all our siblings to your holy table, that we may be connected and nourished for the sake of the world you love.

People: Amen.

Participants begin eating

---

2 Evangelical Lutheran Church in America, 95.

3 As mentioned above, these texts should be selected to speak to the unique group of people who have gathered for this meal. Language to introduce these texts should be added here and/or prior to the usage of each text during the message portion of the liturgy.

EATING AND MESSAGE

Leading Minister: *[Reading #1: a poem, hymn, video, devotional text, essay, Bible verse, or other text that is appropriate to the context and audience.]*

Leader 8: *[Reading #2, for instance this passage from John 21 or another relevant resource]*: A reading from John 21:9–13: "When [the disciples] had gone ashore, they saw a charcoal fire there, with fish on it, and bread. Jesus said to them, 'Bring some of the fish that you have just caught.' So Simon Peter went aboard and hauled the net ashore, full of large fish, a hundred fifty-three of them; and though there were so many, the net was not torn. Jesus said to them, 'Come and have breakfast.' Now none of the disciples dared to ask him, 'Who are you?' because they knew it was the Lord. Jesus came and took the bread and gave it to them, and did the same with the fish."

Leader 9: *[Reading #3: a poem, hymn, video, devotional text, essay, Bible verse, or other text that is appropriate to the context and audience.]*

Assisting Minister: *[Reading #4: this passage from Isaiah 25 or another relevant resource]*: A reading from Isaiah 25:6–9: "On this mountain the LORD of hosts will make for all peoples a feast of rich food, a feast of well-aged wines, of rich food filled with marrow, of well-aged wines strained clear. And he will destroy on this mountain the shroud that is cast over all peoples, the sheet that is spread over all nations; he will swallow up death forever. Then the Lord GOD will wipe away the tears from all faces, and the disgrace of his people he will take away from all the earth, for the LORD has spoken. It will be said on that day, Lo, this is our God; we have waited for him, so that he might save us. This is the LORD for whom we have waited; let us be glad and rejoice in his salvation."

Small Groups for Conversation

Leading Minister: In the next ten minutes or so, discuss in your small groups what have you heard in this worship service and what is resonating for you or what you are still wondering about.

After about ten minutes, return together as a full group.

PRAYERS OF THE PEOPLE

Assisting Minister: We will now join together in the Prayers of the People. After each petition, we invite you to speak your own word or phrase in prayer aloud. Each petition will end with, "God of abundance," to which the assembly will respond, "connect us, nourish us, lead us."

Leading Minister: Let us pray.

Gracious and everlasting God, we gather around your holy and bountiful table as we lift our voices in thanksgiving, praise, and lament.

For the whole church to which we are called, and for the seminarians, lay people, deacons, bishops, and pastors who serve, we give thanks and praise. We pray for unity among your church, that made bold in your mission, the church may faithfully live out the gospel in the world. We now name our church homes before you: the places we love, the places that form us, and the places we are called in service, that you may bless and sustain them. *(Time for people to speak their prayers into the gathering.)*

God of abundance,

People: Connect us, nourish us, lead us.

Leading Minister: For your beautiful and abundant creation, O God, we sing praises and thanksgiving. For bike trails and mountain paths, for deep skies and brilliant sunshine, for soft night air and open fields, for water that flows freely. Be our guide as we strive to dwell faithfully with all you have created, to love creation as our neighbor and to fight for justice for your beloved natural world. We now name before you the land, water, plants, and sky to which we belong. *(Time for people to speak their prayers into the gathering.)*

God of abundance,

People: Connect us, nourish us, lead us.

Leading Minister: For your human creation, for all people made of the earth, we pray for peace, justice, and healing. We pray that we will be leaders in reducing consumption, that as we desire and accumulate less we may be advocates for all people. We pray for our leaders and all those in authority. Grant wisdom, patience, and humility to all those with power. We now name before you the leaders in our own local and global communities, and the people whom they serve. *(Time for people to speak their prayers into the gathering.)*

God of abundance,

People: Connect us, nourish us, lead us.

Leading Minister: For those who struggle and suffer in body, mind, or spirit during these days, we pray to you, faithful God. We pray for those who are lonely, for those who are sick, and for the many who work tirelessly to care for them. We pray for all the workers of this world, those in the fields and factories, the orchards and stores, around the tables and in the kitchens. We especially pray for those who experience injustice and inequity in their food-related work. We now name before you the people for whom we pray for healing and strength. *(Time for people to speak their prayers into the gathering.)*

God of abundance,

People: Connect us, nourish us, lead us.

Assisting Minister: Almighty God in whom we live and move and have our being, we thank you for your many gifts, trusting that you have heard our prayers in the name of Jesus Christ and in the power of the Holy Spirit.

People: Amen.

Assisting Minister: Lord, remember us in your kingdom, and teach us to pray:

People: Our Father, who art in heaven,
Hallowed be your name.
Your kingdom come,

Your will be done,
On earth, as it is in heaven.
Give us this day our daily bread,
And forgive us our sins,
As we forgive those who sin against us.
Lead us not into temptation,
And deliver us from evil.
For the kingdom,
the power,
And the glory are yours.
Now and forever,
Amen.

BLESSING

Leading Minister: You have been nourished by the abundant love of the triune God in this place. Fed and united, you go forth as beloved members of all God's creation.

Assisting Minister: We go out in peace, in the name of Christ.

People: Thanks be to God!

The gathering concludes with people sharing words of peace and helping clean up together as necessary.

Acknowledgments

FROM BOTH AUTHORS

Thank you to Deacon Laura Gifford, PhD, our editor at Fortress Press, who sent an email about a food theology workshop we led, asking, "Have you ever considered writing a book about these topics?" Thank you, Laura, for believing in this book and for accompanying us through the process.

To the students in our "Invitation to Food Theology" class at Wartburg Theological Seminary in spring 2023 and guest speakers Elizabeth Pynn Himmelman and Chuck Tittle: your conversations, passions, and questions stayed with us as we developed this book. We remember that time with joy. We are also grateful for early feedback about this project that we received from members of a theological writing group that meets regularly in Dubuque, Iowa.

As much as possible, we have asked for explicit permission to tell the stories that appear in this book from the people or church leaders involved, especially when those stories came from memories and experiences without external sources like books or websites. At the risk of producing an incomplete list, we would like to thank these wonderful people for sharing their stories and resources with us and with our readers (listed alphabetically by last name): Rev. Dr. Javier Alanís, Rev. Lisa Bates-Froiland, Rev. Carrie Bayliss, Rev. Jason Davis, Alan Guebert, Rev. Emily Harkins, Dave Jarvis, Charlie Koenan, Jeri Kraver, Lauri Lisi, Rev. Ángel Marrero, Sergio Panelo, Grace Sidor Panelo, Rev. Elizabeth Pynn Himmelman, Chris Seaman, Kate Stierman, Rev. Tobi White, Nancy Wright, Venice R. Williams, and Kayla Zopfi.

Thank you to the friends and family who joined the Food Theology Test Kitchen as recipe testers! Special thanks goes to the following individuals, along with their family and friends who tested with them: Sarah Bjornebo, Barbara Cox, Jen and Hannah Douglas, Marie Fry, Beth and Chris Hoden, Leah Holloway-Nilsen, Carly Jones, Amanda Kelly, Heather Kinz, Audrey Lavender, Lauri and Ken Lisi, Karen Martindale, Julie Palubicki, Linda Rindels, Katie Rude, Abby Stickley, Amalia Vagts, and Amber Wichmann. And thank you to the many others who offered their support and enthusiasm throughout both the book writing and recipe testing process.

The gluten-free, nut-free, soy-free, and vegan Communion bread recipe was originally developed by Rev. Tami Groth, who has graciously permitted its usage in this book. This recipe continues to grow in usage at churches across the country and we are pleased to present it to readers of this book.

FROM KELLIE LISI

First, to Martin, without whom this book would have forever been a dream. Thank you for your initiative, your perspective, and your encouragement. Every time I felt like these were stories and practices that didn't need to be shared, you reminded me otherwise. Your wisdom and calm clarity were the engine of this book, and I've greatly enjoyed the writing process with you. From my master's thesis to our first drafts to our video series to the workbook to this book in our hands—it has been an honor to be on this journey with you. Thank you.

To the readers of *Blackboard Kitchen*, my food blog circa 2009–2013, with whom I first thought critically about the power of community when we gather around food. Those years were formative in my understanding and voice in the world of food and I am thankful to the many friends who joined me on that ride. To my colleagues at Wartburg Theological Seminary, including my dear team in the Department of Vocation and Formation, with whom I am blessed with friendship, collegiality, shared mission, and care. It is an honor and a privilege to work alongside and learn from each of you.

To the many places and communities that have shaped and formed me: Abiding Hope, Rainbow Trail Lutheran Camp, Dakota Ridge High School, Mt. Calvary, Mapleton Expeditionary School of the Arts, Bethany, New Legacy Charter School, Wartburg Theological Seminary, Our Saviour's, the Lutheran Center at the University of Nebraska–Lincoln, St. Mark's, and Holy Trinity. In particular: Norm and the Mt. Cal youth group of the 2010–2014 years for teaching me about hospitality and cooking, and who were by my side for the first Dinner Church experience I ever led; the Wartburg Class of 2020 who not only taught me so much, but who trusted me to create an online Agape meal in place of the graduation banquet we couldn't hold in person; the faculty and staff of Wartburg Theological Seminary who taught me and accompanied me as I crafted my own study in food theology; to Pastors Tobi White and Adam White, along with the cook teams, musicians, worship leaders, and many participants who came alongside my explorations of Dinner Church and food theology in action—it was a gift to learn with you all. To the folks who have not only been constants in my life but who also let me interview them and tell bits of their stories in this book: Jeri, with whom I implore, "Are you safe? Are you sound? Are you whole? Are you well?" which is not only the true theme of this book but also of my entire life; Dave and Nellie, who accompany, love, and create space for so many to grow into their gifts and who did the same for me.

To my family: my Grandma and Grandpa Lisi, who came to the United States from Italy, opened an Italian restaurant in Southern California, and helped me to love pasta and sangwhiches[1] and almond cookies. My Aunt Lou and Uncle Dave, whose Thanksgiving table stretched out of the dining room and through the living room, who

1 A sub-style sandwich made with a loaf of Italian bread, cold cuts, thin slices of seasoned tomato, and strips of crunchy lettuce, pronounced in my grandfather's Italian accent and famous in my house as the very best kind of sandwich.

taught me so much about hospitality and good, good care. All my family, with whom I've gathered around those tables throughout my life. The many friends and family who have come to have dinner with us in our garage, our basement, our backyard, our dining room, and on stools at the counter throughout the years. Marie Fry, my friend who embodies every word from the *Caring for Neighbors* section in chapter 5 and who took good care of me and my family in the time I wrote this book. My sister Jessa, with whom I share much, including our joint love for cooking and growing food from the earth. My mom and dad, who have nurtured, supported, and loved me through every moment. Thank you for always being my biggest cheerleaders. Evie and Nolan, whom I love to cook for, even when you don't like what I make. I love you deeply and absolutely, forever. And Jason. You never let me give up and constantly reflect myself back to me. For your steadiness, your love, and your vision, I thank God for you.

FROM MARTIN J. LOHRMANN

I am thankful to the many congregations who have fed my heart, mind, soul, and strength over the years, especially: Trinity and Christ in Walla Walla, Washington; the campus chapel community of Valparaiso University (Valparaiso, Indiana); St. John's in Oshkosh, Wisconsin; Epiphany in Toledo, Ohio; Hosanna in Grand Rapids, Ohio; Christ Ascension in Philadelphia, Pennsylvania; and Holy Trinity in Dubuque, Iowa. I would not be who I am without you and the holy meals and moments we have shared around so many tables and altars.

This project began during a sabbatical granted by Wartburg Theological Seminary, which provided time and resources to explore my personal, pastoral, and scholarly interests in food theology. I am very proud to be part of this community where learning informs mission and mission leads to learning for the sake of Christ's gospel and the health of the world.

I remain deeply thankful to my cowriter, colleague, and friend Deacon Kellie Lisi for being willing to share her expertise in and energy for food theology. It has been a tremendous pleasure to learn from her and work with her as we developed this project, taught a class at Wartburg Theological Seminary, led food theology workshops, and wrote this book together over the past several years. I look forward to seeing how this project will continue to bear fruit and nourish communities in the future.

Finally, I thank Hilde, Jonah, and Theodore for sharing life with me. The love I have received from you is a treasure I carry with me every day. With you I have been blessed to experience Scripture's promise: "O taste and see that the LORD is good" (Ps 34:8).

Bibliography

Adler, Tamar. *An Everlasting Meal: Cooking with Economy and Grace.* Scribner, 2011.

Ahlstrom, Sydney E. *A Religious History of the American People.* 2nd ed. Yale University Press, 2004.

Augustine. *On Christian Teaching.* Translated by R. P. H. Green. Oxford University Press, 1997.

Ayres, Jennifer R. *Inhabitance: Ecological Religious Education.* Baylor University Press, 2019.

Bosch, David J. *Transforming Mission: Paradigm Shifts in Theology of Mission.* 20th anniversary ed. Orbis Books, 2011.

Brugh, Lorraine S. and Gordon W. Lathrop. *The Sunday Assembly: Using* Evangelical Lutheran Worship, *Volume One.* Augsburg Fortress, 2008.

Bugenhagen, Johannes. *Selected Writings.* Edited and translated by Kurt K. Hendel. 2 vols. Fortress, 2015.

Deressa, Samuel Yonas and Sarah Hinlicky Wilson, eds. *The Life, Works, and Witness of Tsehay Tolessa and Gudina Tumsa, the Ethiopian Bonhoeffer.* Fortress, 2017.

Ellwanger, Joseph W. *Strength for the Struggle: Insights from the Civil Rights Movement and Urban Ministry.* HenschelHAUS, 2014.

Evangelical Lutheran Church of America. *Evangelical Lutheran Worship.* Augsburg Fortress, 2006.

Guebert, Alan and Mary Grace Foxwell. *The Land of Milk and Uncle Honey: Memories from the Farm of My Youth.* University of Illinois Press, 2015.

Gutiérrez, Gustavo. *A Theology of Liberation: History, Politics, and Salvation,* rev. ed. Translated and edited by Sister Caridad Inda and John Eagleson. Orbis Books, 1988.

Inter-Lutheran Commission on Worship. *Lutheran Book of Worship.* Augsburg Publishing House, and Philadelphia: Board of Publication, Lutheran Church in America, 1978.

Jensen, Gordon A. *Experiencing Gospel: The History and Creativity of Martin Luther's 1534 Bible Project.* Fortress, 2023.

Kenny, Amy. *My Body is Not a Prayer Request: Disability Justice in the Church.* Brazos Press, 2022.

Koester, Nancy. *Fortress Introduction to the History of Christianity in the United States*. Fortress, 2007.

Kolb, Robert and Timothy J. Wengert, eds. *The Book of Concord: The Confessions of the Evangelical Lutheran Church*. Translated by Charles Arand, Eric Gritsch, Robert Kolb, et al. Augsburg Fortress, 2000.

Lathrop, Gordon W. *The Four Gospels on Sunday: The New Testament and the Reform of Christian Worship*. Fortress, 2012.

Lindberg, Carter. *Beyond Charity: Reformation Initiatives for the Poor*. Fortress, 1993.

Luther, Martin. *Luther's Works*, American ed. 55 vols. Concordia, and Fortress, 1955–86.

Martyr, Justin. "First Apology." In *After the New Testament: A Reader in Early Christianity*, edited by Bart D. Ehrman. Oxford University Press, 1999.

Melanchthon, Philip. *Loci Communes, 1543*. Translated by J. A. O. Preus. Concordia, 1992.

Méndez-Montoya, Angel F. *The Theology of Food: Eating and the Eucharist*. Wiley-Blackwell, 2012.

Miles, Sara. *Take This Bread: A Radical Conversion*. Ballantine Books, 2007.

Miller, Adrian. *Soul Food: The Surprising Story of an American Cuisine One Plate at a Time*. University of North Carolina Press, 2013.

Nessan, Craig L. *Give Us This Day: A Lutheran Proposal for Ending World Hunger*. Augsburg Fortress, 2003.

Nosrat, Samin. *Salt, Fat, Acid, Heat: Mastering the Elements of Good Cooking*. Simon & Schuster, 2017.

Ramshaw, Gail. *Treasures Old and New: Images in the Lectionary*. Fortress, 2002.

Schmemann, Alexander. *For the Life of the World: Sacraments and Orthodoxy*. St. Vladimir's Seminary Press, 2018.

Scott, Emily M. D. *For All Who Hunger: Searching for Communion in a Shattered World*. Convergent Books, 2020.

Smith, Monica M. "Diversity, Equity, Inclusion, and Justice: Institutional Mission as the Call of the Common Good." In VanLaningham, *Called Beyond Ourselves*.

Solberg, Mary M. *Compelling Knowledge: A Feminist Proposal for the Epistemology of the Cross*. State University of New York Press, 1997.

Taussig, Hal. *In the Beginning Was the Meal: Social Experimentation and Early Christian Identity*. Fortress, 2009.

VanLaningham, Erin, ed. *Called Beyond Our Selves: Vocation and the Common Good*. Oxford University Press, 2024.

Wirzba, Norman. *Food and Faith: A Theology of Eating*. 2nd ed. Cambridge University Press, 2019.

Yackel-Juleen, Mark L. *Everyone Must Eat: Food, Sustainability, and Ministry*. Fortress, 2021.

Scripture Index

Subject Index

Recipe Index